The Common-Sense Guide to Improving the Safeguarding of Children

of related interest

Good Practice in Safeguarding Children
Working Effectively in Child Protection
Edited by Liz Hughes and Hilary Owen
Part of the Good Practice in Health, Social Care and Criminal Justice series
ISBN 978 1 84310 945 7
eISBN 978 1 84642 894 4

Safeguarding Children Across Services
Messages from Research
Carolyn Davies and Harriet Ward
Part of the Safeguarding Children Across Services series
ISBN 978 1 84905 124 8
eISBN 978 0 85700 290 7

Social Work Reclaimed
Innovative Frameworks for Child and Family Social Work Practice
Edited by Steve Goodman and Isabelle Trowler
Foreword by Eileen Munro
ISBN 978 1 8490 520 2
eISBN 978 0 85700 461 1

The Common-Sense Guide to

Improving the Safeguarding of Children

Three Steps to Make A Real Difference

Terry McCarthy

Jessica Kingsley *Publishers*
London and Philadelphia

First published in 2015
by Jessica Kingsley Publishers
73 Collier Street
London N1 9BE, UK
and
400 Market Street, Suite 400
Philadelphia, PA 19106, USA

www.jkp.com

Library of Congress Cataloging in Publication Data
A CIP catalogue record for this book is available from the Library of Congress

British Library Cataloguing in Publication Data
A CIP catalogue record for this book is available from the British Library

ISBN 978 1 84905 621 2
eISBN 978 1 78450 092 4

Printed and bound by Bell and Bain Ltd, Glasgow

MIX
Paper from
responsible sources
FSC
www.fsc.org   FSC® C007785

To Ray, Pauline, Chelle, Anna and Seán

CONTENTS

INTRODUCTION

I am enough, not perfect. Perfect wouldn't be enough.
But I am human, and that is enough.

Carl Rogers

This book focuses on the role of local authority social workers and their managers who are involved in the safeguarding of children, but is also relevant for other safeguarding professionals and those interested in enabling children to be safe and well within their own family.

For many decades in the United Kingdom there has been a political, public and professional focus on how safeguarding practice can be effective in ensuring the best outcomes for children. This has involved developing systems which enable clarity about why children are harmed by their families and finding direct and effective interventions to engage with carers and children in order to address concerns and prevent further maltreatment taking place.

For many reasons, which I will explore in this book, this is incredibly complex and challenging, involving a high cost if unsuccessful and low reward if successful. Significant levels of stress and anxiety lead to uncomfortable and intransigent situations between families and professionals. It is natural to seek to avoid such awkwardness and this can result in ignoring the obvious and focusing on issues which are irrelevant but easy to address. This results in a failure to get to the real root of the issue. In order to maintain self-respect and validity, great effort and complex systems are built to defend from this uncomfortable truth. As with any lack of focus, this can involve considerable effort and energy but with no real benefit.

In safeguarding practice, this lack of focus can take the form of overly long and unfocused assessments and reports. Meetings and discussions can have an unclear purpose with a high level of repetition and duplication. Hundreds of hours can be spent working with a family but may not get to the heart of the issue nor find a clear path to ensure best outcomes for children. At a policy and guidance level, the lack of focus can take the form of thousands of professional development events and bookcases full of research, theory, best practice guidance and procedure.

It is presumed that practice events and publications are intended to make a positive difference to safeguarding practice and children's lives. The processes and systems which control and manage safeguarding practice are often considered to be bureaucratic, cumbersome and repetitive; however, it is also presumed that these were developed with the genuine purpose of improving the service.

There is of course much to celebrate about safeguarding social work practice and a considerable number of professionals are doing a considerable amount to make a considerable difference to the lives of children and their families. The vast majority of workers also appear to be hardworking, diligent and committed individuals. It is common for them to work long hours, skip lunch, work whilst sick and go home exhausted in the evening. This must create significant tensions in personal lives and I am aware of many examples of social workers suffering from physical and emotional conditions which are probably related to the pressure and stress of the job. This must affect practitioners' ability to meet the challenges of safeguarding and lead to long-term sickness and a shortened career.

In media comment on safeguarding, there is often the assumption that the reasons for children not being adequately safeguarded relate to ignorant or ineffectual practitioners who are following ridiculous systems. It is inevitable and understandable that, at times of outrage, the media will seek to outline what should have been done to protect a child and question why this was not evident. This focus on mistakes and missed opportunities is often placed in a simplistic analysis of the problem and fails to see the broader complexity of safeguarding children.

Many attempts have been made to write simple rules, which, if followed, would ensure that social workers adequately protect children. Practice guidance, procedures and protocols attempt to clarify these rules. This approach of expecting simple rules to be followed may be very effective with relatively straightforward situations but many safeguarding cases are highly complex and involve multifaceted problems. For many safeguarding cases, expecting procedure and guidance to result in best outcomes for children could be compared to expecting a picture drawn in a 'join the dots' book to be an interesting and thought-provoking interpretation of an object. There has never been a police drama on TV where the detective solves the crime through stringently following standard operational procedure. Quality safeguarding can only be achieved through inspired and creative thinking, where observing the obvious and accepting the first explanation is unlikely to be sufficient to bring about a successful outcome. This will involve high levels of perseverance, flexibility and sensitivity.

There are very good reasons for a lack of clear focus and exploration in complex cases. Put simply, the task of safeguarding children is an incredibly difficult and demanding one. It is riddled with challenges, dilemmas and conflicts. The fundamental reasons for children being mistreated or neglected almost always relate to their carers' ability, behaviour and lifestyle. These most commonly involve substance misuse, mental illness, learning disability, violent tendencies and criminality. These may be underpinned by very deep-seated and long-term experiences and emotional difficulties. Clearly, recognising and addressing these issues, in order to achieve lasting change and appropriate care of children, is highly demanding. Social workers require high levels of skill, confidence, challenge and support to address these adequately and, for a wide range of reasons, these resources are simply insufficient or uncoordinated.

So, social workers are involved with families who, often for complex reasons, do things or fail to do things which result in children's best interests not being met. The safeguarding intervention normally involves influencing adults, who may be family members or those associated with them, to change their behaviour in order to ensure the safety and welfare of children. This exchange can quickly become very complex and requires delicate and careful handling in order to be effective. The role of parenting is very personal, and offering advice or comment about how this is being exercised is very likely to cause upset and offence. This is true when remarks are made amongst family and close friends, when a well-meaning comment can lead to arguments and fall-outs. The role of social workers is to question, challenge and make comment about the care being offered to children on the act of parenting. From the outset of the relationship, this premise is likely to have a strong emotional impact.

This interaction also occurs within a context of one of the most emotionally upsetting and challenging aspects of human behaviour – the maltreatment of children. As social workers, we have chosen to work in very close proximity to the very acts of child maltreatment which we find so abhorrent. We expect ourselves to investigate and report on the detail of this maltreatment. We expect ourselves to spend time and listen to the accounts of children who have been mistreated. We expect ourselves to befriend, support and work in partnership with those who have mistreated children or who have failed to protect them from another's harm. We expect ourselves to stop this maltreatment from happening or from happening again.

This leads to a fundamental internal conflict for professionals. On one hand we are driven by the wish to satisfy a fundamental instinct to ensure that children are safe and well. On the other hand we work in close proximity with toxic aspects of human behaviour from which, whether realised or not, we wish to be distant.

The difficulty with delivering consistent and effective safeguarding of children therefore relates to the highly complex nature of the task and the challenges, dilemmas and conflicts inherent within it. This can lead to distortions and difficulties in the emotional relationships between professionals and families with considerable levels of stress, anxiety, fear and uncertainty being felt by all those involved with or affected by the safeguarding of children.

It is within this overwhelming and highly charged environment that families and professionals can easily lose their sense of purpose and direction. Misjudgements, over-optimism, incorrect assumptions, confusion and misunderstandings can easily occur and, despite best intentions, the relationships can become ineffective, self-defeating and exhausting.

In this book I aim to help understand and resolve these aspects and to present a direct and straightforward approach to effective practice. I will consider how social workers and their managers can better understand, manage and overcome the challenges, dilemmas and conflicts. I will suggest that with some basic changes to how safeguarding practice is viewed, significant improvements in effectiveness can be achieved whilst preventing social workers becoming 'burnt out' or overwhelmed. In particular I will argue that it is important to develop the passion and enthusiasm of professionals and ensure that there is a clear focus and purpose to all safeguarding interventions.

This book was nearly going to be called *The Road to Oz* as it appeared to be a useful way to outline what safeguarding practice requires. In the story, Dorothy on her journey to the Emerald City, meets three friends. The lion wants *courage*, the tin-man wants a *heart* and the scarecrow wants a *brain*. These appear to be the three key qualities required for the safeguarding of children. We need the *brain* to have the knowledge and skill to think through what needs to be done, the *heart* to ensure that we do this with integrity, sensitivity and humanity, and the *courage* to make it happen, often in the face of fear, uncertainty and resistance. This book aims to capture and reinforce these qualities, which are fundamentally part of the good faith and best intentions of those involved with ensuring the safety and welfare of children.

This is a practical guide rather than an academic volume. There is no long list of references and, whilst various authors and publications are acknowledged, the intention is to maintain the flow of the text and focus on the reality of safeguarding practice. This book is unlikely to be accessible, succinct or helpful by being filled with pages of carefully chosen views and observations of others simply because they support my own position. This book is a therefore a personal statement which is valid or not on its own merit.

I am therefore not attempting to state the ultimate truth about safeguarding practice or provide a radical new set of theories. This is an attempt, based on my experience and observations in safeguarding practice for over 30 years, to set out what seems to be the best way to improve some of the fundamental issues and difficulties relating to safeguarding children.

I will aim to be consistent, clear, coherent, fair and proportionate but this is different from suggesting that I am right. There may be aspects of this book which you totally agree with or totally disagree with. I hope this will generate some reflection, thought or debate. The task of safeguarding children is one which is so important that we can never have enough discussion and challenge. It is my hope that this may assist in some small way to create discussion in order to address and develop our skills and confidence to undertake the best possible practice for children.

For much of my career I have followed the belief that knowing what needs to happen, explaining this clearly and monitoring whether it has happened are central to effecting change. This approach was adopted both in terms of work with families and the management of staff. I am now of the view that this approach was my attempt to be diligent and effective but was fundamentally limited and unlikely to achieve the necessary impact. This directness, whilst partially effective, is unlikely to build and inspire the passion, commitment and motivation required to ensure the safety and welfare of children. This book sets out an approach which aims to find, recognise and develop these positive dynamics in terms of how they relate to families' care of children and social workers' intervention and support. It addresses the quality of relationships, focus on children, clarity of thinking and action required to ensure the safety and welfare of children.

Finally, I would like to restate that social workers, in conjunction with partner agencies, often work very effectively together to achieve real benefits and that the vast majority of safeguarding professionals are genuinely committed to doing the best job they can within the systems and processes which have been developed to support this work. It must therefore be concluded that within the safeguarding environment there is a high level of commitment to address issues and ensure that the best possible service can be developed to safeguard children. This book aims to embrace this commitment, improve understanding of the issues which lead to poor practice, increase the number of children who receive an outstanding service and identify cost-efficient approaches to achieving this.

TERMINOLOGY

'Child' refers to anyone under 18 years old.

'Carer' refers to any adult or young person who has a responsibility to care for or meet the needs of a child. This includes parents, step-parents, partners, siblings, members of the extended family, friends, temporary carers, guardians and those living in the child's household.

'Social worker' refers to a local authority employee with a recognised qualification, who has lead responsibility for planning and service delivery to children and their families.

'Children's services' are local authority departments which focus on working with children and their families.

'Safeguarding' refers to ensuring the safety and welfare of children is protected and promoted.

'Safeguarding professionals' are practitioners and their managers from all safeguarding agencies.

'Partner agency' refers to an organisation that works with children's services to address the safeguarding of children.

'Safeguarding services' are statutory and voluntary organisations which offer services to address the safety and welfare of children.

'Safeguarding environment' refers to the activities and motivations of safeguarding professionals, family members, those associated with the family, referrers and other individuals involved in the care and safeguarding of children.

BACKGROUND AND CURRENT ENVIRONMENT

The level of need and risk

The safeguarding systems in the UK are generally considered to be among the best in the world and have been used by many countries as a template for developing their own systems. Across England and Wales fewer than one in a hundred children are either looked after (in care) or the subject of a child protection plan and there are only about one in five hundred children where legal proceedings have been initiated by local authorities.

In addition, safeguarding agencies intervene, or should intervene, where children are '*in need*', as defined by section 17 of the Children Act 1989, meaning that their health and development is being impaired. Estimates for how many children are '*in need*' vary enormously but it is suggested that this is likely to be in the region of 1 child in 30.

So, any problems regarding the safeguarding of children do not affect the vast majority of children, who appear to be cared for in a reasonably appropriate manner and do not require the intervention of safeguarding services. Indeed, raising children to be healthy and safe has been a basic objective of societies since the earliest history with neglect, cruelty and maltreatment of children consistently being seen as a social taboo. Whilst methods used to care for and discipline children are sometimes questionable in hindsight, the overall intention consistently appears to relate to raising children in the best possible manner to become fully functioning adults.

At the opposite end of the scale, a very small proportion of carers will very seriously mistreat their children and, on rare occasions, this may result in the death of a child. The National Society for the Prevention of Cruelty to Children (NSPCC) estimates that, in the United Kingdom, 50 to 100 children are killed by their carers each year. This is a very subjective figure as the vast majority of these deaths do not result in criminal proceedings. The reasons why carers seriously harm or kill their children will be as varied as the number of incidents and no system could probably ever be developed which would effectively address these.

To expect safeguarding services to prevent all child deaths could be compared with expecting the police to solve all serious crime or a medical surgeon to have no fatalities. Such expectations are unrealistic and unreasonable. Instead, the role of safeguarding services can be seen as being vigilant and responsive to situations where a child appears to be mistreated and to ensure that these are investigated and monitored, leading to necessary action to ensure the child's safety and welfare.

Since the birth of the welfare state following the Second World War, there have been fewer than 40 child death public enquiries. The most recent and prominent of these include Graham Bagnall (who died in 1972), Maria Colwell (who died in 1973), Jasmine Beckford (who died in 1984), Tyra Henry (who died in 1984), Kimberley Carlile (who died in 1986) and Victoria Climbié (who died in 2000). The importance of these enquiries has been such that many of the names, even many years later, are still very familiar to safeguarding professionals and the public. Over the last 15 years the political pressure to hold public enquiries has reduced, so that deaths such as Peter Connelly's (Baby P who died in 2008) did not lead to a public inquiry.

Messages and lessons which have been identified

In examining why some children are not adequately safeguarded, it should be emphasised that there is probably no easy answer. If there was, this would almost certainly have been identified and resolved a long time ago. Serious harm to a child may relate to bad timing, involving a critical moment when a number of events coincide or impact on each other. To understand why children are not adequately safeguarded, many elements need to be considered in terms of how they act both in isolation and in combination to undermine or prevent effective safeguarding practice.

In addition to public inquiries, there have been thousands of case reviews and inspections of children's services which have highlighted messages and lessons relating to how safeguarding agencies can ensure the safety and welfare of children. On the whole, these messages and lessons have focused on three key areas.

The first key area relates to **practice issues**, including:

- lack of clear purpose and focus
- vulnerable children and their families not being seen in a timely manner

- care plans being unclear and failing to address the real problem
- risk factors not clearly being understood or responded to
- delays in assessing need or risk and in offering services
- lack of an historical perspective and insufficient use of chronologies and case summaries
- insufficient consideration being given to the family's background and culture
- lack of engagement with families and their extended network
- safeguarding professionals not having sufficient knowledge about child development
- insufficient attention being given to the impact of the situation on the child
- children in the family getting overlooked, with an over-emphasis on particular siblings or carers
- information and evidence not being adequately analysed or evaluated
- insufficient use of theory, research and effective interventions
- inadequate direct involvement with children
- willingness to accept the explanations of carers
- compliance and cooperation being seen as evidence of good parenting
- over-optimism and over-keenness to give families another chance
- lack of clarity relating to visits and professional meetings
- interpreters and culturally sensitive services not being used
- care plans not being robustly reviewed to ensure they are being followed and are effective
- insufficient consideration being given to hospital admissions, medical opinions and discharges
- consideration not being given to the welfare of children who are being cared for by those who do not have parental responsibility
- insufficient and inadequate resources being made available to children and their family
- delays in using police protection and legal intervention

- information presented to court proceedings being outside timescales and not clearly identifying risks
- individual failings and errors.

The second key area relates to **inter-agency communication**, including:

- failure to communicate effectively, with key information not being shared, understood or taken into consideration
- lack of understanding between agencies with regard to systems, processes and thresholds
- professionals having different views and these not being fully explored or resolved
- a tendency to accept the views of other agencies, particularly if they are perceived to be of higher status or authority
- inability to challenge views and information
- children not being referred to agencies in a timely manner
- referrals not being adequately acknowledged, discussed or responded to
- insufficient resolution to conflicting medical opinion
- lack of adequate joint training across agencies.

The third key area relates to **systems and strategic structures**, including:

- agencies not ensuring information is conveyed regarding families who move between local authorities
- lack of focus on children who do not attend school
- not identifying children who fail to be registered with a school or family doctor
- lack of robust supervision and monitoring of front line practitioners and managers
- inadequate training for front line practitioners and managers
- senior managers and elected members lacking strategic vision and involvement
- insufficient overview and challenge from local safeguarding children boards (formerly known as area child protection committees).

These issues appear to continue to be relevant. In October 2014, Ofsted published a summary of inspections held under the framework implemented in November 2013. Of the 33 inspections undertaken, 18 children's services were judged to 'require improvement' and 6 were judged as 'inadequate'. Most of the issues, as highlighted above, are to be found in the 33 Ofsted reports relating to these inspections.[1] In the 3 years up to 2013, Ofsted inspections found 13 per cent of local authorities to be 'inadequate' and 47 per cent to be 'adequate'.[2] The latter would be assessed as 'requires improvement' under the inspection framework implemented in 2013. Virtually all of the messages and lessons from the last 60 years, as summarised above, are also found in the Ofsted evaluation of serious case reviews which was undertaken in the four years up to March 2011.[3] These reviews relate to situations in which children were harmed or placed in serious danger and safeguarding agencies thought that lessons could be learnt from studying and analysing the involvement with the family.

Ofsted inspections and publications of serious case reviews lead to regular reports in the media relating to safeguarding practice failing to effectively safeguard children. Each year we can expect to see several high-profile stories of children being seriously harmed or killed by their carers. These are likely to trigger debate about the safeguarding of children and can lead to expectations, commitments and initiatives to address identified issues.

Attempts to address these messages and lessons

The above messages and lessons have provoked significant political, public and professional debate and led to considerable pressure on central and local government to identify the reasons for poor safeguarding practice and develop initiatives to reduce or eliminate the likelihood of this reoccurring. The following are some of the main attempts over recent decades to achieve this.

Legislation, training and publications

There has been a significant amount of legislation and government regulation, supported by practice guidance, procedure and protocols, to identify what is expected of social workers. Research and development of theories have informed and influenced best practice. In addition, there has been much focus on the training and development of safeguarding professionals with countless conferences and courses being attended.

Most training and publications tend to emphasise what social workers *should* be doing to safeguard children and the legal, theoretical and research basis for this. The emphasis therefore appears to have been on providing more information and direction based on an assumption that practice will be improved if professionals are clearer about what they should be doing. Whilst this may be partially true, consideration also needs to be given to the barriers and issues which lead professionals sometimes not to meet requirements with which they are familiar.

Monitoring practice

Monitoring practice has increasingly been a focus for all safeguarding agencies, with considerable performance information being produced to meet management, publication and central government requirements. This information is normally reviewed by managers on a regular basis in order to monitor how legal and procedural requirements are being met.

Performance monitoring tends to focus on quantitative aspects of activities, for example the number and timeliness of visits, meetings, supervision and assessments. It is less likely that it will address the quality of these activities and whether they are effective in ensuring the safety and welfare of children. This is more likely to be achieved through the use of qualitative monitoring approaches such as case analysis, auditing, practice observation and consultation with service users. These are very resource intensive and require careful planning if they are to improve safeguarding practice. Issues relating to quantitative and qualitative monitoring will be explored in detail later when it will be argued that a combination of these approaches is required to identify and address issues and ensure best practice.

Reviews, enquiries and investigations

As already indicated, there has been an increasing number of serious case and internal management reviews into specific cases where performance or outcomes were considered inadequate or have caused concern. Since 2010, local authorities have been required to give consideration to publishing full serious case reviews and *Working Together to Safeguard Children* (2013) strengthened this requirement, meaning that virtually all serious case reviews will become available to the public. This will undoubtedly lead to increased exposure of safeguarding professionals and agencies to public and media examination. Much of this can be expected to be 'headline grabbing' and superficial. However, the availability of these reports also offers an opportunity for a more reflective and serious exploration of the issues.

There have also been major national reviews of safeguarding services. The most significant of these recently has been *A Child Centred System* in 2011, also referred to as the Munro Report, which will be discussed in detail shortly.

National campaigns

There have been many high-profile national campaigns led by major charities and government departments, for example 'Quality Protects', 'Every Child Matters', 'Safeguarding is everyone's business' and the NSPCC 'Cruelty to children must stop. Full Stop'. These have aimed to change the safeguarding environment through addressing public attitudes, practice issues, processes and systems. They have reflected broad concerns about how children can best be safeguarded and raised public awareness. In the case of charities and voluntary organisations, these campaigns also represent an important aspect of their public profile and are often linked to requests for financial support.

New social work models

There have been a number of new models introduced which aim to address practice issues. The Signs of Safety model, developed by Andrew Turnell and Steve Edwards, was based on an Australian model and is used in many child protection conferences. It aims to balance a focus on risk to children with highlighting protective factors in order to identify an action plan which is built on cooperation between professionals and the family.

Some children's services have adopted the Reclaiming Social Work model which focuses on practice using the 'McKinsey 7S model', which considers strategy, structure, systems, shared values, skills, style and staff. Central to this model is a redesign of social work teams to include a range of skills and professional approaches to collectively consider risks to children and how these can be addressed in conjunction with partner agencies and the family.

Professionalisation of social workers

In order to raise the status and recognition of social workers, over the last 20 years the social work qualification has moved from being a *certificate* to being a *diploma* to being a *degree*. Additional training has been made available to safeguarding professionals through central government funds and the reprioritising of local financial resources. Post-qualification courses are available to social workers who have also been required to register with professional bodies. With the establishment of the Health and Care Professions Council (HCPC) in 2012, the government is attempting to be more robust in ensuring that social workers meet standards and can evidence this in their continuing professional development profile. Failure to do so can lead to professional registration being removed, which prevents them from legally being employed in a social work position.

The context of safeguarding

Safeguarding practice exists within the context of a complex social, financial and political environment which has a major influence on safeguarding professionals' ability to ensure the best outcomes for children. The following are some of the key elements which appear to be currently impacting on safeguarding practice.

Lack of resources and 'austerity' measures

Lack of resources is very commonly highlighted as a key contributory factor to the difficulties in delivering effective safeguarding services. It is undoubtedly true that over recent decades resources available to most safeguarding agencies have reduced in real terms. Indeed, some of the highest performing children's services and partner agencies appear to be better resourced, with social workers having at their disposal more than an average range of projects and initiatives.

Over recent years the financial pressures on safeguarding agencies and services have increased significantly. For example, local authority funding is expected to have reduced by 43 per cent over the period 2010–2015.[4] In some authorities the core safeguarding functions within children's services have been protected from reductions in resources. However, safeguarding practice relies heavily on a wide range of agencies, many of which have been significantly reduced in their numbers and scope over recent years. This has meant that core safeguarding services have been left with significantly fewer resources to draw on for support and assistance.

For example, since the London bombings in 2005, the Metropolitan Police's key priority appears to be the prevention of further attacks and this has resulted in less police resource being available to child protection conferences and child abuse investigation teams. Also Women's Aid report that, due to reductions in resources, refuges are unable to assist on average 150 women each day, the majority of whom are accompanied by children. This is likely to mean that many of these women and children will return to violent and abusive homes.[5]

Charities are also under considerable financial pressure with some estimates suggesting that one in six are in danger of closure or considering merging with other charities in order to survive. Other services particularly affected by reductions in resources include family support services, children's centres, youth provision and advocacy services.

The Care Quality Commission confirms that health visitors, school health advisors and midwifery staff are under increased pressure to meet health priorities with most having increased caseloads and pressures.[6] Whilst safeguarding is still clearly considered a priority, overstretched services can mean a struggle to attend meetings, support families and commit to specific aspects of child protection plans. These pressures on agencies may also affect the timing, nature and process of making referrals to children's services. Whilst many referrers are happy to retain their role, some referrals may relate to managing demand through transferring responsibility for a family over to children's services or other agencies. This can undermine the principle of joint responsibility with referrals creating tension between agencies.

In most safeguarding agencies, reduction in resources has taken the form of leaner administrative support and management structures. This can lead to overstretched management structures and inadequate administrative support, resulting in less support, capacity and guidance for practitioners.

Austerity measures have also affected social workers on a personal level with reductions and freezes in pay being endured over many years. This has probably added to the sense of being unfairly treated with many agencies, particularly children's services, having difficulty retaining staff. This in turn has increased the number of agency staff which has added further stresses in the form of unstable teams and wage differentials between temporary and permanent staff.

It would seem reasonable to conclude that resources are a real issue affecting how safeguarding agencies address the safety and welfare of children. There appears to be a shift of responsibility towards children's services, which is increasingly seen as the key agency responsible for safeguarding children. In real terms there are continuously decreasing resources available to meet the needs of vulnerable children. The key challenge appears to be how available resources can best be focused and utilised to ensure the maximum benefit to children.

Poverty

As confirmed by the Institute of Fiscal Studies in 2013, the social structure of the United Kingdom has shifted with 3.1 million people and 600,000 children now considered to be living in poverty.[7] Reductions, in real terms, in family benefit systems have placed significant financial pressure on many families. The introduction of the 'bedroom tax' and benefits being capped has meant that some families are having to move out of their current homes to more affordable properties. The increase in membership of the European Union and freedom of travel have also probably meant there are many more families entering the United Kingdom who find themselves isolated, destitute and vulnerable. This can create massive pressure on safeguarding agencies, particularly children's services, when these families have no recourse to public funds or when financial and social problems affect carers' ability to adequately care for their children.

Research by Bebbington and Miles in 1989 found that children who came from socially disadvantaged families, as defined by income, family size and accommodation, are up to ten times more likely to require involvement of statutory safeguarding agencies.[8] It seems likely that the increase in the number of low income families may at least partially explain the increases in referrals to children's services, child protection investigations, assessments, legal proceedings, children looked after and children who are the subject of child protection plans.

As confirmed by the National Institute for Health and Care Standards (NICE), the pressure on families due to lack of money can also lead to an increase in the use of drugs and alcohol.[9] This can have an impact on children because of the carer's lifestyle choices to gain money, shortage of funds to provide for the children and impaired levels of caring due to the effect of these substances. Partially related to this is the increase in domestic disputes, which can easily lead to violence and a harmful environment for children. Mental health and emotional problems are also closely linked to financial income and the availability of opportunities to make a positive contribution through activity and work.

These issues relating to substance misuse, relationships, criminality, violence, mental health and emotional difficulties, which are at least aggravated by poverty, are a significant contribution to the increased complexity of safeguarding practice.

Lack of a clear purpose and social expectation

It is tempting to think that there is a clear focus and purpose which all social workers can relate to, but there are conflicting demands and expectations from the public, politicians, agencies and others involved in social policy. Issues relating to how children should be cared for are riddled with social contradictions. For example, when he was Prime Minister, Tony Blair openly admitted that he had 'smacked' his child, however he did not appear to feel that there would be a public outcry and he may have felt that he was speaking for the views of many carers. Other countries have made physical chastisement illegal or have developed definitions of what is acceptable. There is no such clarity in the UK.

Issues relating to the rights of privacy and carer's rights often confuse the context of safeguarding and set up alternative priorities to the safety and welfare of children. This can be clearly seen in the public debates around adoption over recent decades. The balance has regularly swung between the rights of children to have the best adoptive match to the rights of prospective adopters not to endure prohibitive requirements and intrusion.

The image of safeguarding professionals, and social workers in particular, has also been subjected to contradiction and inconsistency in the media and public debate suggesting that there is a lack of clarity about the role and expectations of professionals. For example, social workers are at times portrayed as being over-eager to interfere in family life, with moral arguments being put forward to protect privacy and the rights of carers. At other times social workers are portrayed as ineffectual and unable to intervene to protect children. This is often summarised as 'damned if you do and dammed if you don't'. However, what is not clearly identified is the space between these two extremes within which professionals are expected to practise.

Public, political and court pressures

Since the mid-1970s, there has been an increasing expectation that public bodies will be transparent and accountable. This has involved them being open to scrutiny, with individuals having the right to be heard and challenge decisions. Whilst greater openness and challenge must be welcomed, it also places safeguarding practice in a more complex and challenging environment. For example, up to the early 1980s service users had very limited rights to make a complaint and no access to records relating to them which were being held by professionals. Both of these are now considered to be fundamental aspects of enabling service users to have a voice and engage on equal terms. Over recent decades there has also been increased involvement of elected councillors and members of parliament taking up service-user dissatisfaction and monitoring social workers.

Changes in public accountability are arguably most significant in relation to legal interventions and the use of civil courts. Up to 1992, with the implementation of the Children Act 1989, local authorities could assume parental rights and duties (under Section 3 of the Child Care Act 1980) for children who were in 'voluntary care'. This assumption of parental rights and duties was effectively a care order granted by elected councillors, often based simply on a report from a social worker. Carers had no right to either challenge this application or formally present their wishes and feelings. They could appeal the local authority decision but this was a complex process, which required a high level of motivation.

Since the 1990s, applications to courts, under children's legislation, have become increasingly lengthy, complex and costly, with higher levels of evidence and process required. This led to the implementation of the Public Law Outline (PLO) in 2008 which requires children's services, if there is no immediate danger to a child, to meet formally with families to discuss concerns. There are also requirements to complete significant amounts of assessment and care planning prior to making an application to court.

The new Ofsted inspection framework, introduced in November 2013, further increased the focus on outcomes for children, how agencies are working together and the experiences of families. These inspections follow a short period of notice and are more intensive than previous arrangements. The re-categorisation of 'adequate' to 'requires improvement' is a clear indication that the new arrangements expect children's services to be 'good' or 'outstanding'. Early indications are that over half of children's services are being judged as 'requires improvement'. It is important that challenge is balanced with support to enable learning and change. Given the focus and resources available to Ofsted and safeguarding agencies it appears unlikely that this support will be sufficient, with the consequence that inspections will be experienced by agencies as attacking and demoralising.

Structural and strategic direction

Since the beginning of the century, there has been a growing acceptance that poor safeguarding practice is partially to do with how safeguarding practice is overseen by senior managers, political leaders and strategic bodies. The Laming Report (2003)[10] into the death of Victoria Climbié concluded that there was a 'gross failure of the system', agencies 'gave a low priority to the task of protecting children' and were 'poorly led'. Councillors and senior managers were criticised in the report for stating that they were 'strategic' and therefore not involved at a practice level.

The Laming Report led to significant changes to structural and strategic arrangements for child protection, including the relationship between central and local government and how agencies work together to safeguard children. For example, the report led to changes relating to:

- the role of government ministers and their departments
- how agencies are inspected and regulated
- how senior managers and elected members monitor cases and provide leadership and overview
- the creation of statutory local safeguarding children boards
- how local authorities work together with families who move between them
- the development of client databases.

The Laming Report also examined the ways in which agencies fail to work together effectively to refer children, share information and consider the welfare of a child from a number of agencies' perspectives. The report highlighted the tendency of agencies to focus on their own role with a family without giving adequate consideration to what other agencies are doing. A common analogy is to see this as being like a jigsaw with each agency holding some of the pieces but no agency having a clear vision of the overall picture.

In the decade following the Laming Report there was a significant shift in how senior managers, elected members and strategic bodies coordinated and oversaw safeguarding practice. This led to an increase in joint working and co-location, with agencies working together more closely to deliver effective multi-agency services. There were also examples of agencies jointly funding and managing resources, which resulted in increased efficiency in service delivery and use of resources.

Ofsted reported, in 2013, that there is a 'persistent absence of stable leadership' in local authorities considered to be 'inadequate'.[11] In a pressured environment and when there is a danger that safeguarding practice may not be given adequate priority, it therefore continues to be important that chief officers and political leaders ensure there is clarity about the focus of agencies, the development of partnerships and how safeguarding is placed within wider agency priorities.

Processes and central government 'prescriptions'

Following the death of Peter Connolly (Baby P) in 2008, there was much discussion about whether there are fundamental problems with safeguarding systems and processes. The government commissioned Professor Eileen Munro to examine systems and practice failures which may have led to Peter Connolly's death. The findings of the review were published in the 2011 report *A Child Centred System* (referred to as the Munro Report). This report identified aspects of central government and safeguarding agency expectations which appeared to be blocking the flow of best practice. The report recommended a re-balancing to enable a more flexible and locally determined approach to safeguarding within a national framework.[12]

The Munro Report was an important examination of how practice can become unfocused with social workers being confused between *process* (the tasks required – for example, visits, meetings and report writing) and *outcomes* (the benefits to children). This was believed to have led to social workers spending too much time and energy ensuring that tasks are completed without examining the impact these were having on children's lives.

The report focused on two key systems which had been developed and implemented by central government across England and Wales. These were the *Integrated Children's System* (ICS) and the *Framework for the Assessment of Children and Their Families* (referred to as the Assessment Framework). These systems had been introduced to address the lack of robust assessment, and recording and planning. The Munro Report also recommended changes to *Working Together to Safeguard Children* (2010), which, whilst offering national guidance on safeguarding, was thought to have become too lengthy and detailed.

These systems and guidance were also identified as examples of central government having become too 'prescriptive' of safeguarding practice. This appeared to contribute to social workers not taking responsibility and control of their own practice, thus restricting creative, reflective and effective intervention. Many of the formats in ICS and the Assessment Framework were considered to encourage a one size fits all and tick box approach. Reports and recording required under these systems often involved significant levels of duplication and could make it difficult to organise information into a coherent picture of the family, identifying why a child was being harmed and what was required to address this. This may have contributed to practitioners often not being able to differentiate between key and background information leading to often lengthy, unfocused and repetitive documents. These could lack clear focus and purpose and therefore fail to clearly identify the needs of the child and risks to their safety and welfare.

It should be remembered that the level of government prescription was a response to national concerns, supported by the Laming Report, to develop a framework to establish a clear, focused and effective national system for safeguarding children and monitoring practice. The changes were an attempt to address significant practice issues and therefore unlikely to have *caused* the lack of focus, creativity and child-centred practice identified by the Munro Report. It is easily argued that the systems and processes were cumbersome, repetitive, bureaucratic and poorly designed. Despite this, it would appear reasonable to conclude that the systems and government prescriptions were well-intentioned, if unsuccessful, attempts to address the crisis of safeguarding acutely felt at the end of the 1990s.

Caution needs to be exercised before believing that returning to more locally autonomous systems will be a move to better safeguarding practice. There has never been a golden age of creative, reflective, child-centred and effective safeguarding which has eroded or been undermined over the last decade. There is no evidence that old paper files and various locally developed assessment models, which predated ICS and the Assessment Framework, led to a better quality of intervention. As Olive Stephenson reported in 1993, '...there is an urgent need for those who work day to day at field level in child protection to develop and apply a more sophisticated level of analysis and intervention'.[13]

There is sometimes a view that ICS and the Assessment Framework have kept practitioners at their desks and away from direct contact with families. However, as reported by Unwin and Hogg in 2009, practitioners spent 80 per cent of their time on administrative work.[14]

It should be considered that the issues which led to ICS and the Assessment Framework and identified by the Laming and Munro Reports relate to more fundamental aspects of safeguarding practice which need to be identified and addressed before progress can be made. It is worth noting that the Seebohm Report in 1968 found many key issues relating to practice which are still very familiar today. The report remains a significant watershed, having established social services departments, a professional qualification and the title of 'social worker'. The report observed that:

- workers were demoralised by 'bad press' and unable to do an effective job

- there was a climate of reducing resources

- services needed to be more flexible, focused, facilitative and supportive

- families required a clear message about acceptable standards of parenting.[15]

This demonstrates that the issues relating to effective safeguarding practice are historic and therefore probably relate to cultural issues rather than being caused by initiatives or changes which have taken place over the last two decades.

Following the Munro Report, there has been a shift towards local authorities having more autonomy and central government being less prescriptive. Examples of this are the shortening of *Working Together to Safeguard Children,* national timescales for assessments being modified and greater flexibility being allowed about how ICS and the Assessment Framework are implemented.

Professor Munro published a *Progress Report: Moving Towards a Child Centred System* in 2012, which considered the implementation of her previous recommendations. In this report she stated that 'progress is moving in the right direction but that it needs to move faster'. She particularly welcomed developments relating to Ofsted's inspection framework, early intervention, selection processes for social work training and government data requirements.

The current environment

Safeguarding practice has therefore undergone considerable examination and a wide range of political, strategic and procedural interventions. It is important to consider the impact of this activity and scrutiny on the current environment of safeguarding practice before focusing on how practice can be developed.

Stress and pressure on social workers

A recent social worker survey found that the current average career of a social worker was eight years.[16] This raises significant issues for sustaining a quality professional workforce with so many practitioners feeling unable to commit to a long-term career.

This highlights that probably the greatest risk to effective safeguarding practice and the welfare of staff relates to them working under high levels of stress, anxiety and uncertainty. As will be explored, there are many areas of challenge, dilemma and conflict which contribute to these pressures, but it is also worth considering more broadly the likely consequences of working in an emotionally demanding environment.

Stress is normally associated with situations where there are high levels of anxiety or uncertainty. This is often simplified as relating to the 'fight or flight' response, which means that under these conditions individuals go into overdrive to enable them to confront the risk or escape from it. This affects many aspects of physiology including raised levels of blood pressure, heart rate, adrenaline and stress hormones. This can lead to the body being inhibited from physically repairing itself and resolving emotional issues, potentially causing illness and exhaustion.

Stress can be used to describe many aspects of life and most people will experience levels of stress which are not necessarily unhealthy. However, long-term or chronic stress can lead individuals to being continuously in a state of heightened vigilance and emotional arousal, whilst becoming desensitised to the effects which this can cause. This can result in a wide range of health symptoms including headaches, fatigue, anxiety attacks, stomach complaints, depression and insomnia. The medical profession accepts that chronic stress is a contributory factor in many illnesses, with some estimates suggesting that is could be as high as 90 per cent. Chronic stress can also lead to behavioural and social issues such as eating disorders, poor relationships, addictive behaviour, substance misuse, poor concentration, accidents and poor judgement.[17]

The high level of stress and pressure on social workers can lead many to feel demoralised, overwhelmed, out of control, anxious, fearful, uncertain and frustrated. With large caseloads in many agencies there is often a sense of too much work being expected of too few. This can lead to long working hours, high sickness levels and high turnover of staff with staff vacancies, creating a vicious cycle of pressure. A survey undertaken by the British Association of Social Workers (BASW) in 2013 found that 77 per cent of social workers felt they had unmanageable caseloads with 46 per cent stating that they felt afraid of the repercussions if they raised the issue with their manager.[18]

Over recent years there has been a rise in the use of hot-desking, which involves individuals having no fixed work station. This has mainly been driven by the need to maximise office space to reduce costs. There are some advantages to hot-desking, including improvements in communication and less chance of teams or individuals becoming isolated or marginalised. However, at times of uncertainty and stress, social workers can place a greater importance on the stability and predictability of an office environment which provides opportunities for formal and informal support groups to be established. Hot-desking can have a negative impact on this and may affect an individual's ability to manage pressure.

There is a danger that high levels of stress will lower the performance of social workers. The long working hours, which are common to many practitioners, may not proportionately increase productivity as it is generally accepted that effectiveness drops with overwork and tiredness. For example, a task which may take an hour at the end of a long day, may take half this time when a practitioner is fresh. There is also the risk of errors and misjudgements leading to additional work and stress.

The relationship between practitioners and families

Social workers feeling stressed and overwhelmed can also have a significant impact on their involvement with families. In this environment, practitioners can easily develop 'tunnel vision', being too focused on particular aspects and failing to identify risk factors, gather key information or find effective ways to address the situation. There is an increased likelihood of practitioners becoming too involved with peripheral issues or being unable to offer challenge or raise difficult matters. This may involve unwisely accepting explanations or commitments from families and believing that there is progress even if this is not supported by evidence.

Crucial to effective safeguarding practice is the ability to be vigilant, proportionate and honest with families. The level of judgement required for this is less likely when social workers are under stress or feeling overwhelmed, which may lead to defensive behaviour. As already considered, this can take the form of being process driven rather than focusing on the outcomes for children. Alternatively, some social workers may respond to the stress by being overly punitive or interventionalist which can result in alienating families or lead to inappropriate practice, making future engagement more difficult. The likelihood or reflective and creative thinking is also significantly reduced, and practitioners are less likely to be open to new ideas, practice issues and being challenged.

The risks of these factors will be most significantly felt with complex families, who are difficult to engage or hostile to agency involvement. With these families the practitioner is particularly likely to feel stress and pressure. However, it is here that engagement and clarity are particularly important in ensuring the safety and welfare of children.

The relationship between practitioners and managers

The relationship between practitioners and their manager has long been considered an important aspect of achieving best practice. Ideally this would involve the practitioner gathering information, coming to an analysis of risk or need and making proposals to their manager about how these can be addressed. The manager will consider the quality of information, analysis and the proposed plan. This process ensures that the case is viewed from at least two angles, reducing the likelihood of an error or inappropriate interpretation. This is where consideration is given to cases which are complex or confusing to ensure that effective approaches are identified. This process of constructive discussion is a crucial part of a practitioner's learning. It is also where management decisions, for example to escalate a case to a legal planning meeting, can be made so that accountability for the case is held by the agency as a whole.

However, difficulties can arise when social workers feel stressed or overwhelmed and this leads to them becoming isolated or anxious. This can cause the relationship with the manager to become unhealthy and ineffective, perhaps with the practitioner avoiding their manager or providing them with limited or distorted information. Alternatively, some practitioners may become over-reliant on their manager for direction and guidance. In either of these scenarios the relationship between the practitioner and manager is less likely to involve reflective and creative thinking, managerial scrutiny and an opportunity for the practitioner to develop their confidence and skill.

Many managers find it difficult to have the time to be able to explore constructive discussion on cases. For example, caseloads in many social work teams are high and this is generally recognised to have an impact on the quality of work which a practitioner can offer. Less recognised is the multiplication effect on the manager who may have up to seven social workers reporting to them. This can seriously restrict the manager's ability to offer guidance, challenge and support. With limited time available in formal supervision to discuss cases in detail, much discussion takes place informally, which raises issues about the nature and quality of the discussion, recording and monitoring of practice.

Focusing on process rather than outcome

As discussed, safeguarding agencies place a high priority on performance indicators which monitor practice and whether the agency as a whole is offering an appropriate service. For example, children's services' performance focuses on activities such as responses to referrals, timescales for completing assessments, timeliness of conferences or reviews and the regularity of visits, core groups, recording and supervision.

When under pressure and stress it is common for individuals to focus on prominent expectations and those things which are most likely to cause difficulty if not completed. In this context it can be understood why there may be too much focus on those activities which are being monitored, leading to practice being driven by process rather than outcome. As already seen, this focus on process rather than outcome was highlighted by the Munro Report as a key difficulty for safeguarding practice.

The tendency for success to be measured through performance indicators can also define the nature of the relationship between practitioners and their managers. The limited time for case discussion, as discussed, can mean that it is based around the manager being directive about activity and processes rather than being able to have a more qualitative discussion relating to engagement with the family and outcomes for children.

Professionals who are feeling anxious or vulnerable may also have a tendency to seek anything which provides a feeling of control and predictability. Processes and procedures, for example relating to ICS and the Assessment Framework, can often meet this need and provide a sense of reassurance and certainty in an overwhelming environment. Entering information onto a computer system provides the comfort of a warm, secure and predictable office environment with trusted colleagues. This may be preferable to the often hostile, challenging and uncertain environment of direct contact with families.

Conclusion: Developing direct effective safeguarding

So there are considerable areas of pressure on the safeguarding environment, which may contribute directly or indirectly to why, on occasions, safeguarding practice fails to adequately identify and address the risks to children.

In addition to concerns about children being seriously injured, ineffective safeguarding practice also has a direct impact on a vast number of children who will never come to the attention of the public, an inquiry or inspectors. These children continue to live in unacceptable and unhappy situations and are almost certainly suffering physically and emotionally in the short term and possibly in the long term. Their continuing neglect and maltreatment are very likely to have a life limiting effect as a child grows up without the quality of care, security and safety they require to become responsible adults. In addition to the unhappiness experienced during childhood, this can lead to a cycle of abuse with an increased likelihood that they become adults who are unable to offer appropriate care to their own children.

Some of the key elements which impact on effective safeguarding practice are:

- pressures on safeguarding agencies at times of reducing resources
- emotional stresses experienced by safeguarding professionals who often feel overwhelmed
- financial, emotional and social pressures experienced by families
- deep-seated carer lifestyles and problems which are leading to children being mistreated or neglected
- carers who are difficult to engage and may be evasive or defensive
- lack of clear and consistent public and political expectation
- the impact of considerable change and policy initiatives
- too much focus on procedure and task rather than outcomes for children.

Successful safeguarding practice involves ensuring that issues relating to the safety and welfare of children are identified and addressed effectively. This requires a wide range of considerations, including:

- developing constructive relationships, including building rapport and trust
- enabling, supporting and challenging family members
- engagement with partner agencies
- actively exploring issues and probing behind the obvious
- identifying the history and background of the family
- considering the relevance of ethnicity, race and religion
- considering disability issues
- interpreting why and how events have occurred
- considering an individual's motives and judging their commitment
- ensuring that there is a focus on the experience of the child and that the ultimate outcome is in their best interests

- ensuring early intervention, which is more likely to be effective
- ensuring timely intervention and immediate risks are addressed
- being flexible, analytical, reflective and creative
- understanding the principles behind practice
- making professional judgements which are proportionate, balanced and fair
- being open-minded to all possibilities, including the most unacceptable, abhorrent and difficult to comprehend
- being evidence focused and open to research and theory which informs best practice
- recognising and utilising strengths and protective factors
- understanding and exploring the nature of risk and need
- considering the impact of root problems (fundamental reasons for maltreatment) and risk factors on the child
- considering how change can most effectively be achieved
- recognising the emotional impact of safeguarding
- continuously gathering and analysing information, views and commitments
- being solution focused and forward thinking to ensure the safety and welfare of the child
- planning clearly and ensuring progress in relation to root problems and risk factors, within reasonable timescales
- having management overview and consideration of necessary action, including legal intervention.

This list highlights the incredible challenge of safeguarding practice. Achieving this ideally requires professionals and families to be in a relaxed and calm working environment, which enables focus, clear purpose and relationships which support change. However, the challenges of safeguarding practice can lead to high levels of stress, anxiety, fear and uncertainty for both professionals and families, which can directly affect levels of morale, energy, confidence, knowledge and skill.

Amongst safeguarding professionals, the pressure to achieve best practice is probably felt most acutely by social workers, who are expected to hold key responsibility and coordination for cases. Whilst normally supported by partner agencies, social workers are often expected to carry a disproportionate accountability for monitoring, assessing and planning. To some degree this is appropriate as it is the local authority children's services department which is responsible for deciding if a child is suffering or has suffered significant harm and for taking legal action or deciding whether a child will become looked after. The social worker is also the key coordinator in the professional network and normally the main point of contact with the family.

It should be emphasised that in most situations the complexity and demands of safeguarding practice do not lead to a child being placed at unacceptable risk or being seriously harmed. The important point is that, with such powerful conflicts and pressures, there is always a significant possibility that practitioners, particularly social workers, may not maintain a focus on risks to a child and that this may contribute to a serious incident occurring.

When this does occur, safeguarding agencies are likely to be held accountable for failing to recognise the risks and not intervening in a timely and effective manner. It is unusual for the complex elements, as outlined above, to be carefully considered. In the emotionally charged environment which follows a child being tragically harmed or killed it is more common for individuals to be singled out for public attention and punishment. This was seen to happen following the two most recent high profile child deaths of Victoria Climbié and Peter Connolly.

The remainder of this book focuses on the assumption that the complexity of practice can be better understood in order to find a series of measures which are effective in addressing each aspect of safeguarding practice. The culmination of these measures can make a massive overall difference to the outcomes for children.

A helpful analogy for this approach to improvement is the success of David Brailsford, who became the performance director of the Great Britain cycling team in 2004. The team had just won four medals at the Athens Olympics. Four years later, at the Beijing Olympics, the team won 14 medals, including 8 gold medals. At the London Olympics in 2012 they achieved a similar number of medals and were the top performing team in the world. Brailsford's approach was also behind Bradley Wiggins, in 2012, becoming the first British person to win the Tour de France.

Brailsford's approach, which he refers to as the 'aggregation of small margins', was not to find a radical new approach but to recognise that each part of the process could be slightly improved and collectively this would make a significant difference. To achieve this, every aspect of the bicycles, helmets, diet, training regimes, etc. were dissected, analysed and redesigned.

In a safeguarding context, this approach would suggest that a series of relatively small and achievable changes can have a significant cumulative effect. The following three steps will be explored to focus on how these changes can be identified and undertaken. With each of these steps, actions are suggested which will address key aspects in a straightforward and achievable way.

Step One: Establish a culture which enables and leads

Fundamental to ensuring the best outcomes for children is the development of a culture which has clear purpose and focus. This should support the identification of risk to children, develop a plan to address these risks and ensure that this plan is progressing within reasonable timescales.

Consideration will be given to developing healthy and effective relationships which have clear expectations and are based on respect, courtesy, trust, empathy and valuing others. The work with families must involve practitioners and managers feeling motivated, energised and in control of their tasks and duties. This will require strong communication with other professionals and family members, accepting that both progress and challenge are natural aspects of positive interaction. It is important that there is a clear understanding of the use of authority, which is inherent in relationships between carers and children, professionals and families, and professionals and managers. This authority involves a balance between, on one hand, understanding and being sensitive to the wishes and feelings of a range of individuals and, on the other, making decisions, perhaps uncomfortable to some, which are considered to be in the best interests of children.

A healthy culture is considered to be one where professionals and families are supported to learn through creative and reflective thinking, recognising that this that can sometimes involve mistakes, misjudgements and relapses. Confidence and courage are necessary to ensure that these are actively used as part of the change process whilst not placing a child or other person in unacceptable danger.

It is also important that there is close monitoring of practice and performance to ensure that risks to children are being adequately identified and addressed. As identified in the Munro Review, information based purely on *quantitative* performance information can only provide a limited picture of this. Auditing and monitoring the *qualitative* aspects of practice is crucial to ensuring effective intervention, learning and decision-making.

Step Two: Develop a stable, skilled and confident workforce

It is presumed that most social workers are hardworking and dedicated practitioners who are reasonably clear about *what* should be done and *why* this is required to safeguard children. They often struggle, however, with *how* they can bring about the required outcomes, often because they lack the skill or confidence to overcome the complexity, challenges and conflict inherent in safeguarding children. This can result in social workers being 'process driven' – committing considerable energy and resources without this necessarily leading to the best outcomes for children.

Practitioners and managers are often affected by anxiety and fear, which can lead them to feel overwhelmed. This can affect their ability to have a clear focus, engage with families, identify risks and think creatively/reflectively. Twenty areas of emotional challenge, dilemma and conflict for professionals will be identified which will need to be understood and managed if they are not to have a negative effect on practice.

It is important that children's services have a clear framework for recruiting, appraising and developing social workers. It will be proposed that this should be based on an expanded version of the nine competencies developed by the College of Social Work/Social Work Reform Board with an additional eight skill sets for team managers.

Managing, monitoring and supporting professionals to develop skills and confidence require a blend of supervision, coaching, training, consultation, auditing and practice guidance. This must be undertaken in conjunction with partner agencies, finding approaches which, even with reducing resources, ensure that professionals contribute and work together to share accountability for the safety and welfare of children. Discussion with partner agencies is likely to focus particularly on how and when referrals are made, how assessments are undertaken, the role of core groups, evaluation of information and decision-making. This may require clear systems and processes for resolving conflict and disagreement and ensuring that children's services are not isolated when making key decisions.

Finally, it is important that professionals are not at risk or undermined by unacceptable and abusive behaviour from family members. Suggestions will be made on how to reduce the likelihood of this occurring and how incidents of unacceptable behaviour can be addressed.

Step Three: Enabling families to change

Effective safeguarding practice requires social workers to establish direct and effective work with families, in conjunction with partner agencies, in order to ensure children are safe and well. In order to do this there must be a continuous process of assessing and planning – evaluating risks to children and finding solutions to address them.

In order to develop this continuous cycle of evaluating risk and finding solutions, with positive relationships between professionals and families, 13 areas will be outlined. These will involve ensuring there is a clear understanding of root problems and risk factors, there are plans in place for addressing these and there is evidence that progress is being made to address the root problems and risk factors. If change cannot be achieved within reasonable timescales, decisions will need to be taken to ensure the children are safe and well.

It is suggested that work with the family is structured around solution-focused practice, which explores and identifies the changes that need to be made and the benefits. In this way the family remains positive and motivated to address the root problems and risk factors. This will require effective and direct relationships with families and partner agencies in order to support families to address necessary change. It is important that there is clarity about how meetings with the family, core groups and other contacts are focused to ensure that key aspects of the plan are progressed.

The skill of managers is important in ensuring that the best interests of the children are met. Practitioners will require guidance and direction in relation to issues arising on their cases. It is important that formal and informal supervision take place, which allows sufficient time to discuss all cases to the level of detail required. The manager's involvement should focus on the progress being made to ensure the safety and welfare of children and to make necessary decisions – for example, convening a legal planning meeting – if acceptable progress is not being made.

How the three steps work together

Whilst these three steps may all influence each other, it is important to see them as sequential. This means that if Step One is not achieved it is unlikely that either of the following two steps will be achieved. Similarly, if Step Two is not achieved it is unlikely that Step Three will be successful. It is of course this final step which is the crucial goal of effective safeguarding of children. This does not mean that achievements in Steps One and Two should not be recognised and celebrated. The important point is to see them as intermediary stages along the way of enabling families to change, ensuring the safety and welfare of children.

David Brailsford may have felt a great achievement when a reshaped helmet carved a few milliseconds off a lap time but not because of a commitment to develop better quality equipment. Instead he would have seen this as a useful step in achieving his ultimate focus and purpose – his cyclists winning races. Similarly, the development of a strong culture, clear leadership, skilled workforce or professional partnerships is only of value when they contribute to real and lasting positive change in families relating to the care and protection of their children.

STEP ONE

Establish a Culture which Enables and Leads

This first step in achieving effective safeguarding for children is ensuring that there is the environment or culture which enables the right attitudes and relationships to develop between those who are involved in ensuring the safety and welfare of children. This means establishing and maintaining a clear set of values, principles and beliefs which influence and determine behaviour and interactions. In simple terms a culture can be defined as 'the way we do things round here', relating both to what is considered to be important and how this is achieved.

A safeguarding culture is considered to involve the relationships which take place between children, carers, practitioners and managers. The concepts below, which make up a healthy culture, should be understood as needing to be embraced by all of these groups and the relationships which take place between them. For example, the relationship between managers and social workers will most likely influence how social workers relate to carers, which in turn will influence the relationship between carers and their children. This is often referred to as modelling or, put more simply, leading by example. Building attitudes and relationships is crucial to ensuring a culture which, using a common currency of interaction, ultimately leading to a positive and constructive outlook that ensures the safety and welfare of children.

As will be examined, there are many aspects which will lead to this. However, in general terms an effective safeguarding culture will:

- treat individuals with respect, value and dignity
- enable learning and change
- be fair and equitable
- have a clear purpose and focus

- be clear about how the purpose and focus will be achieved
- develop and support effective approaches and practice
- aim to consistently achieve best outcomes for children.

The following are some of the key elements to be considered in order to develop and maintain an effective culture which enables and leads.

Ensuring the best interests of children are met

At the heart of any effective safeguarding culture is ensuring that the involvement is focused on the best interests and outcomes for children. Whilst each individual will have a unique set of values and beliefs which motivate them, it is crucial that central to these is a clear focus on how they can ensure the safety and welfare of children. Clearly, the fundamental premise of safeguarding practice is that it involves carers who are considered to have failed to appropriately meet the best interests of their children, have given them insufficient priority or have ignored or denied their experience. Many carers may struggle with understanding how their actions have harmed their child and may find it upsetting to realise that they have done so. Much of safeguarding practice is therefore related to clearly identifying how a child is believed to have been mistreated, what is in the best interests of the child and how this can be achieved.

From a professional perspective, whilst it may seem obvious that the best interests of the child should be at the centre of the work, lessons from recent decades have consistently shown that the child's experience is not always adequately considered. Serious case reviews, Ofsted inspections and inquiries have shown that assessments, plans, conferences and interventions have often insufficiently acknowledged the impact on children or failed to take into consideration their views, feelings and experiences. This was one of the key messages from the Munro Report, which strongly argued that safeguarding professionals have been unable to consistently develop and maintain focus on the best interests of children.

Some professionals who are primarily providing a service to carers may have views about the child's best interests but presume that this will be the focus of the child's social worker. Indeed, even those professionals who are directly involved with the child may tend to expect the social worker to engage with the child in order to identify their views, feelings and experiences for the purposes of assessing and planning. The following sections will therefore particularly focus on the role of the social worker with regard to how they can ensure that the best interests of children are met.

Why the best interests of children may not be met

It is important to consider the dynamics which may prevent professionals ensuring the best interests of children are met. First, keeping the safety and welfare of the child at the centre of the intervention can be in conflict with engaging with carers and addressing their needs. The maltreatment or neglect of children is almost always linked to the circumstances and needs of carers, for example due to them having violent tendencies, being victims of maltreatment, suffering domestic violence, having a learning disability, experiencing mental health problems or being dependent on substances. This can lead to the intervention focusing too heavily on the carer and therefore insufficiently on the child. The approach may be justified on the basis that the child will benefit if the needs and issues of their carer are addressed. However, it may not necessarily lead to a significant improvement in the child's safety and welfare.

For example, the professional may believe that the neglect of the child relates to her mother's dependence on alcohol. The professional may therefore be supporting the mother's access to counselling and a substance misuse programme. Once progress has been made, the crucial question is whether it results in her offering more stable and appropriate care to her child. This requires safeguarding professionals to remain focused on the child, whilst the work is taking place with the mother, in order to identify whether the intervention is improving the child's safety and welfare. If it is not then consideration should be given to whether the neglect of the child relates to other issues. It may be that the neglect is not caused directly by the alcohol dependency but rather the neglect and dependency both relate to deeper emotional issue. If this is not identified and addressed it is unlikely that the care of the child will significantly improve.

A second reason why the best interests of children may not be met relates to some social workers not having values and attitudes consistent with ensuring that the child best interests are at the heart of the work. There may be many reasons for this and, as will be explored, it may be possible to assist the practitioner to address their purpose and identity in order to become more child centred. If this cannot be achieved then the practitioner can have a seriously negative impact both in their own cases and on their service as a whole. It is therefore important that these practitioners are identified through supervision, case monitoring and staff appraisal with consideration given to whether the social worker is suitable for safeguarding practice. It is also important that recruitment interviews focus on what motivates prospective employees.

Finally, the best interests of children may not be met due to the complexity and challenge of engaging children in direct work. This involves the views, feelings and experiences of children being understood and considered as part of assessing and planning. These children, many of them very young, are very likely to have suffered from the acute or chronic effects of neglect and physical, sexual or emotional abuse. They may have witnessed traumatic incidents and the unpredictable behaviour of their carers due to the impact of violence, substance misuse or mental illness. This contributes to children being in a constant state of upset, anxiety, fear, confusion, uncertainty and insecurity. Children can also be very confused or uncertain about safeguarding agency involvement and will often be defensive towards family members.

Given these circumstances, it is understandably difficult and emotionally challenging for practitioners, most commonly the social worker, to focus on children's views, feelings and experiences and to develop a relationship with them. This will often require considerable patience, perseverance, creativity and resilience in order to develop a rapport. It will also involve considerable time and effort, both in terms of the hours spent with the child and the weeks which may be required to build trust and communication. In the time-pressured world of safeguarding it is perhaps not surprising that some social workers will therefore avoid or marginalise their involvement with children.

Benefits of focusing on the best interests of children

Despite all these difficulties and dilemmas it is important to ensure that children are at the centre of the work and that social workers receive the support and challenge to enable them to ensure that they overcome these issues and persevere with ways in which they can spend time with children to gain insight into their views, feelings and experiences. Practitioners must become sensitive to the day-to-day reality of the child in order to understand the impact of the maltreatment or neglect. It is not sufficient for practitioners to know the theory and research relating to the likely long-term consequences of maltreatment and neglect, but rather they should understand how this uniquely effects each child.

The most immediate benefit of focusing on the best interests of children and gaining insight into their views, feelings and experiences is that it is important in understanding and determining risks to the child and in identifying a plan to address these. In the absence of a focus on the child, it is inevitable that a partial analysis will be developed based on the perspectives of adult family members and partner agencies.

A second benefit of focusing on the best interests of the child is that it enables social workers and partner agencies to maintain a clear purpose in their intervention. Most professionals state that their motivation to undertake safeguarding practice relates to addressing the fundamental unfairness and cruelty to children. In order for safeguarding professionals to develop their skills, approach and confidence, it is important that they remain focused on this motivation. Direct involvement with children and focusing on their views, feelings and experiences is a very effective means of ensuring a clear connection with a sense of professional purpose. This can significantly improve the likelihood that the safeguarding intervention will be underpinned by an understanding of the risks to the child, ensuring their safety and welfare.

Finally the views, feelings and experiences of children are probably the most accurate indicator of whether the intervention with the family is being successful. The time and energy spent working directly with children can therefore significantly influence the intervention and prevent months of ineffective involvement. Issues relating to direct work with children will be explored further in Step Three.

Developing learning and positive change

An important aspect of enabling and leading is ensuring that the safeguarding culture supports and encourages learning, growth and development. The resulting positive change should be considered in terms of both professionals and families.

Social workers will be involved in learning and change, developing their skills and confidence to be able to offer an effective service to families. As will be explored in Step Two, there are a number of ways in which learning and change can take place and it is crucial that practice on all cases meets the agency's expectations, particularly in terms of ensuring the safety and welfare of children. At an individual level this will involve identifying strengths and areas of professional development. At a broader level it is important that learning and change take place within an environment which supports individuals in exploring issues and learning from each other's experiences, skills and approaches.

Families are involved in the learning and change process to ensure that they are enabled to reflect on their current situation and choices, considering the benefits of developing new skills, behaviour and lifestyle. In a safeguarding context this should result in the improved care of children. It is likely to be motivated by the intervention of agencies, and at the heart of all learning and change is clarity of purpose in terms of the nature of the intervention and how change will be achieved. It is therefore crucial that families understand what is expected of them or 'what good looks like' before any effective learning is likely to happen. As with the development of safeguarding professionals, support and guidance are important in enabling this learning to take place.

Using theory and research

Important to learning and change is being aware of key theory and research which inform safeguarding practice. Chris Beckett defines theory as 'a set of ideas or principles used to guide practice, which are sufficiently coherent that they could if necessary be made explicit in a form which is open to challenge'.[19] Theory and research are important ways to recognise patterns, predict future behaviour and identify interventions which are more likely to be successful. A sound knowledge of theory and research will therefore assist in identifying issues which require further exploration and discussion.

Developing new approaches has become important in safeguarding practice and this has led to extensive research into a range of programmes, for example the Signs of Safety model and parenting programmes, with the effectiveness of these approaches being scrutinised and refined. As a result, there has been increased use of programmes which have been shown to be effective, with improved clarity about which approaches are likely to be most appropriate in particular circumstances.

Theory and research can also be very useful in persuading individuals of their need to address behaviour and lifestyles. For example, it is common for families to feel that domestic violence does not affect children if they have not been directly injured. Theory and research clearly demonstrate that children tend to be aware of carer disagreement and violence and this can have a profound and long-term impact on children. This can include increased likelihood of lifelong relationship difficulties, mental health problems, substance use and criminality. It can be very helpful if these findings are shared with carers in order to reinforce the reasons for concern and to motivate them to address these.

Whilst theory and research can be very valuable, it is also important to remember that most effective safeguarding intervention is based on straightforward, incontrovertible truths and ensuring that interventions are focused on addressing these. The Laming Report emphasised this principle when it advised that safeguarding professionals should 'do the basics well'. Whilst theory and research may assist in this, they can also confuse and alienate. It is therefore important that practitioners are influenced and inspired by theory and research and find engaging ways to incorporate important ideas into their work with families. Theory and research provide a set of precise ideas. However, these need to be balanced with the creative and reflective process of developing healthy and effective relationships with families based on respect, trust, empathy and understanding of their specific circumstances.

Feedback

The process of learning and change can be significantly enhanced if an individual is able to receive constructive feedback. R.D. Laing stated that 'the range of what we think and do is limited by what we fail to notice. And because we fail to notice what we fail to notice, there is little we can do to change'.[20] This demonstrates the importance of being observed and having the benefit of astute feedback and information in order to assist individuals develop insight and understanding of their behaviour and how this may lead towards or away from their objective and purpose.

Feedback can involve elements of support and challenge, both of which are important if learning and change are to take place. It is important that there is an appropriate balance between support and challenge. If there are low levels of support and high levels of challenge the feedback is likely to be experienced as attacking, which can lead to demoralisation. Alternatively, if there are high levels of support and low levels of challenge the feedback is likely to be ineffectual and may not enable learning or change to take place.

In order for feedback to be effective there should be agreement about its purpose and how challenge and support will be used. Permission to offer feedback is important and this should be reconfirmed at key points throughout the relationship. Crucial to constructive feedback is the intention to meet the recipient's objectives and learning goals with the focus being on the benefit to the person receiving the feedback. Constructive feedback is therefore most likely to occur when there is clarity about an individual's strengths and areas of development, for example from an appraisal undertaken as part of their continuing professional development.

A very useful technique in assisting an individual see their own patterns is to reflect back to them what they are saying and doing. This requires the enabler to be a skilled and sensitive listener – they must not add to the information, emphasise aspects of it or judge it either positively or negatively. The enabler is simply a mirror which allows the individual to see their own behaviour, assumptions and beliefs in a clearer light so that they are able to make their own choices about them. It is advisable to do this gradually and to check whether the reflection is accurate and helpful. An extension of this approach is to ask the individual to listen to and comment on themselves as if they were a third party. This can assist the individual to view their own behaviour and outlook objectively and enable them to recognise the impact they are having on others.

Safety to make mistakes, relapse and be 'stuck'

Crucial to learning and change is ensuring that individuals are supported to feel reasonably safe and relaxed while being challenged and supported to develop. Learning and change tend not to follow a straight line from not having knowledge, skill or confidence to being competent. It should be recognised that there may be setbacks along the way.

Good learning involves the ability to manage and overcome mistakes, relapses and feeling 'stuck', realising that these are a natural part of learning and change. In school classrooms, when effective learning is taking place, teachers sometimes reward and celebrate mistakes and encourage children to be open about when these occur. They are encouraged to regard feeling stuck, frustrated or confused and the process of overcoming these feelings as important aspects of learning. This may involve developing the ability to look at an issue from other angles, ask a different question or break a situation down into smaller parts. Having support and assistance to do this is important.

Many theories about change support the idea that the process does not run smoothly. Prochasta, Norcross and DiClimente's model of change emphasises that 'relapse' is one of the five stages of change. They point out that this can be the stage at which individuals are likely to consider the process a failure and give up. Instead, it can be seen as a point to re-contemplate the issues and to learn further about what action will be required to successfully reach the objectives. In this way relapse can be seen as an inevitable part of the cycle of change.[21]

Colin Carnall sets out five stages of organisational change which involve a range of feelings and responses. The *denial* stage involves a belief that change is not necessary, leading to high morale and performance. The *defence* stage involves a realisation of the need for change, leading to a drop in morale and performance. The *discarding* stage involves frustration and hopelessness as old systems and skills are no longer being used, leading to a further drop in morale and performance. The *adaptation* stage involves new systems and skills starting to be understood and incorporated, leading to increased morale and performance. Finally, the *internalisation* stage involves new systems and skills being fully understood and incorporated, leading to a high point in morale and performance.[22] This model illustrates that a healthy process of change involves periods, particularly during the defence and discarding stages, when frustration and low morale may be felt. If not fully understood, this can lead to periods when individuals may consider their situation is getting worse, leading to a temptation to give up and terminate the attempt to change. Whilst Carnall's model relates to organisational change, the stages described are also relevant to personal change.

These inevitable mistakes, relapses and feelings of being 'stuck', associated with the process of learning and change, relate both to safeguarding professionals and families as either may act in a manner which involves repeating a mistake or falling back into unhelpful behaviour. However, this can be very useful in finding out more about the learning and change which is being attempted and identifying what can be taken from the situation to assist in better understanding the barriers to change and how they can be overcome. In this way, the likelihood of their reoccurring can be reduced and new approaches developed based on analysis of what has happened. It is crucial that this is undertaken with a spirit of learning and development rather than criticism and blame.

The idea of making mistakes is a difficult one in a safeguarding context as they are often considered dangerous, potentially leading to undesired outcomes for children, complaints and criticism. Clearly, some issues are too sensitive or important to allow mistakes to be made and it is the role of safeguarding agencies to ensure that, through clear expectations and monitoring, mistakes do not lead to serious harm to a child or another individual. It is important for social workers to know at what point they may be making a decision which requires consultation and the agreement of an appropriate manager or specialist. Similarly, certain behaviour or mistakes by a carer may result in serious harm to a child and it is important that monitoring and vigilance reduce the likelihood of this happening, identify increases in risk and take necessary action if an undesired event does occur.

When considering the possible consequences of mistakes it may be helpful to consider the analogy of a circus high-wire performer. A novice would not practise their routine twenty foot off the ground where a mistake could prove fatal. Instead they would initially practise with the wire a few inches off the ground or whilst in a safety harness. In a similar way, it is important for practitioners and their managers to have a clear sense of the practitioner's level of skill and experience so that appropriate monitoring and guidance can be offered. This requires careful judgement, as too much monitoring and guidance can restrict the development of confidence and creativity while insufficient monitoring and guidance can mean there is an unacceptable level of risk. Safeguarding professionals should feel able to take an acceptable level of appropriately judged risk and use this to learn and develop their skills and confidence.

Carers must also be enabled to develop confidence and skill in ensuring the safety and welfare of their children. This may involve developing new parenting skills or making new lifestyle choices and, in the process, mistakes, relapse and being 'stuck' are very likely. The level of monitoring and guidance should enable, rather than restrict, the process of change but at all times the consequences of these mistakes must be kept within acceptable limits.

Most practice, however, does not involve this level of danger and whilst mistakes may be undesirable they can normally be accepted as part of the process by which professionals or families are developing, persevering and attempting to find effective ways to ensure the safety and welfare of children.

Creative and reflective thinking

The issues above are important in considering how creative and reflective thinking can be developed in practice, as proposed by many, including the Munro Report. Creative and reflective thinking by their nature involve taking risks and trying something which may be new or where the outcomes may not be certain or predictable. If the safeguarding culture is risk-averse, meaning that mistakes are seen as always to be avoided, then creative and reflective thinking simply cannot develop. The important issue is to ensure that the risks or uncertainty are at an acceptable level and that a mistake or misjudgement, if it does occur, would not be disastrous.

It is helpful to consider the idea of 'flow', which is used in schools to define an enabling atmosphere where students can be absorbed and committed to a task. It is described by Griffiths and Burns as 'the glue that binds all previous elements together…the fertile soil which enables sustainable learning to take root and flourish'.[23] This flow is how children explore issues, take risks, develop ideas and take actions, becoming independent learners within a stimulating environment.

Creativity and reflection are of course not the same as anarchy, and it is important that thinking takes place within clear parameters which define objectives and expectations. Professionals and carers should clearly understand the guidance, procedure, regulations and organisational expectations and ensure that they are always respected. It is not always necessary to follow these to the letter and it should be remembered that practice guidance, procedures and regulations are often advisory. This means that they should generally be followed unless there are good reasons not to do so. In this event it is necessary to ensure that a manager is aware of the deviation from common practice expectation and the reasons for doing so. As the Munro Report highlights, it is important for social workers to understand the principles underlying practice guidance, procedures and regulation. In this way professionals will be in a better position to understand what level of deviation from common practice is appropriate in a particular situation.

The process of learning and change

On a personal level, most people have experience of attempting to make changes in their lives, normally with varying levels of success. Common examples of this relate to wanting to lose weight, stop smoking, reduce alcohol consumption or address financial debt. These probably relate to the majority of New Year's resolutions and it is common for these to lead to some short-term progress but not bring about long-term change. There are several reasons for this.

First, intention is often expressed in terms of current behaviour and not what is being sought. This means that the focus is on the problem – for example, smoking, being overweight or financial overspending. This has the effect of holding in the mind the behaviour which the individual is attempting to change, causing a tendency to move towards that behaviour or even reinforcing it. This is due to behaviour, which relates to basic needs, being controlled by a primitive part of the brain, often referred to as the 'reptilian' brain. This functions like an animal's brain, which is unable to appreciate negative concepts or the ironic. So whether one says to a dog 'We are going for a walk' or 'I am not taking you for a walk' or states either of these in a sarcastic tone, the effect will be the same. The dog will only hear the part relating to a walk and start heading for the front door. Another example of this effect is that when someone is told *not* to think of a pink elephant they see the image of a pink elephant. So if the undesired behaviour is kept in mind, for example by thinking 'I must stop smoking', a part of the brain is holding onto the image of being a smoker.

Focusing on the behaviour to be changed also means being conscious of what is being lost – for example, the food, cigarettes or alcohol and to which there is likely to be an emotional attachment. When focusing on these behaviours there is a tendency to consider them in connection to personal deficiencies such as being foolish, greedy or lacking self control.

This self-criticism is very likely to have an impact on confidence and undermine the belief that the behaviour can be changed. This means that the change process is often entered into with no strong emotional conviction about the desire or ability to succeed.

New Year's resolutions are often linked to a belief that willpower or determination will result in change. Indeed, it is very common for behaviour to change during the month of January. For example, membership and attendance at gyms increases significantly during this period. However, as gyms will confirm, their usage by March returns to a level similar to the previous December's. This illustrates how willpower can be very effective for several weeks, after which the tendency is to revert to the old behaviour. The main reason for this is that willpower takes considerable effort leading to tiredness which, in combination with inevitable periods of weakness, tends to lead to seeking comfort, which is often most easily found in the undesired behaviours. It is sometimes stated that 'if you can change a habit for a month you can change it for life' and this may be due to a likelihood that such change is being driven by something more substantial than willpower.

A further element which may contribute to change not being successful relates to the lack of recognition that most behaviour is emotionally driven, whereas decisions to address these are often based on logical considerations. Neurological research shows that emotional and logical thinking are controlled by different parts of the brain, meaning that logical thinking is unlikely to address or change emotionally driven behaviour. For example, if an individual eats comfort food because they feel unhappy it is unlikely that this behaviour will change if the motivation is based on logical reasons for losing weight, such as being healthy and living longer. The individual may therefore require counselling or support to understand the basis for their behaviour before change is likely.

Attempts to change which do not prove successful often cause feelings of failure, making it more difficult to try again to change. This can lead to feeling trapped in the behaviour, with negative effects on confidence.

Success in changing behaviour is significantly improved if the target is linked to a strong motivational factor. This is more likely to happen if the change is stated in terms of the purpose and benefits being sought. So, instead of thinking of being on a diet or stopping smoking, the focus should be on the target of 'becoming healthier', 'living longer' or 'becoming more active'. This provides an immediate incentive and reason for change which can be linked into consciously and unconsciously. These aims are more likely to focus the mind on the destination and benefits of change and therefore are more motivating and encouraging.

In a safeguarding context, to enable change it is therefore important to concentrate on what is desired rather than focusing too strongly on the problem. When working with families, concerns must be identified in terms of risks to children. However, a careful balance should be struck by clearly identifying what outcomes are required, for example appropriate care or protection of a child. Similarly, enabling safeguarding professionals to change will involve being clear about what is expected of them and supporting individuals to achieve this. In both of these situations the emotional dynamics must be explored in order to ensure that these do not prevent change taking place. These issues will be considered further in Steps Two and Three.

Motivation to change

In order to further explore what leads to effective change, it may be helpful to examine the levels of neurological motivation based on the work of Robert Dilts.[24] The four levels, as outlined below, are in order of their strength of influence on an individual, with purpose and identity being the most powerful motivational factor.

- *Purpose and identity* relate to what an individual sees as their core mission, passion and reason for life. This is closely associated with self-image and how an individual fundamentally defines themselves, including key values and strongly held moral, religious, spiritual, social and political beliefs. These are the issues which, in extreme circumstances, lead them to endure discrimination, attack, persecution and even death rather than give up their sense of self. Beliefs, skills, knowledge, behaviour and environments, as discussed below, can often be inconsistent with purpose and identity, and the process of change involves highlighting these contradictions and supporting the individual to develop more balanced lifestyle choices. In a safeguarding context, it is reasonable to presume that the safety and welfare of children is a central aspect of carers' and safeguarding professionals' purpose and identity. This sense can of course become lost due to conflicting considerations or lifestyle. However, assisting an individual to understand and connect with their purpose and identity can be crucial in motivating real and lasting change.

- *Beliefs* relate to how situations are viewed, what is considered to be important and judgements about what is acceptable. They relate to attitude and are more changeable and flexible than the underpinning purpose and identity. In a safeguarding context it is important to identify beliefs as these can be very useful in assisting individuals to make choices about what they should do and develop understanding about how they can meet their purpose and identity.

- *Skill and knowledge* are normally developed to enable an individual to satisfy their beliefs, and purpose and identity, leading to frustration or unhappiness if these cannot be met due to a lack of skill and knowledge. In a safeguarding context an important aspect of change is for individuals to recognise and develop skills and knowledge which will ensure the safety and welfare of children.

- *Behaviour and environment* relate to habits, relationships and situations, and it is important that these enable the development of skills and knowledge which in turn fulfil a person's beliefs, purpose and identity. If they are involved in behaviour, relationships or environments which are not leading them towards their purpose and identity then they are likely to feel frustration and unhappiness. The process of change involves assisting an individual to recognise these conflicts and to make new choices regarding behaviour and environment.

Attempts to change lifestyles are often considered to relate to aspects of behaviour and environment. For example, becoming healthy may involve taking on new behaviour and changing social circles. They may also involve developing new skills, for example taking up a sport or developing some new beliefs relating to health and fitness. These changes may have some impact but there is a significantly greater chance of successful long-term change if consideration is given to how purpose and identity can be also engaged. For example, an individual may decide to run a marathon to raise funds for a valued cause. The motivation to become fit is now linked to purpose and identity. This shift is very powerful because it means an individual sees themselves in deeper terms of *who they are* rather than the relatively superficial *what they do*.

Enabling others to change

So in order for behavioural change to take place, consideration should be given to the positive objectives and emotional reasons behind the behaviour and levels of motivation. These all relate to conceiving the change and developing a clear vision of what is required. However, this may not be sufficient for change to take place if an individual does not feel confident and able to make the change.

Enabling others to change therefore also relates to how individuals are assisted and supported to develop their sense of purpose and identity, beliefs, and skill and knowledge so that they can achieve the confidence to address their behaviour and environment. It involves encouraging individuals to find their own answers and take responsibility for their own choices about how they act or think. In this way they are placed at the centre of their own decisions and are fully committed to them. This supports the process of learning and the development of confidence and resilience. In a safeguarding context, examples include:

- a child who is enabled to address their behaviour

- a carer who is enabled to end a violent relationship which is placing their child at risk

- a social worker who is enabled to be more direct and honest with carers

- a social work manager who is enabled to address their style of supervision.

The role of the enabler is to be non-directive and to support the individual to make decisions which *they* feel are appropriate, based on *their* own purpose, identity and beliefs. This is an example of how communication, trust, value, dignity and respect can be demonstrated between two individuals. The process of enabling involves guiding an individual and encouraging them to self-reflect rather than directing or taking over responsibility for making decisions. This involves assisting an individual to consider the type of person they need to become in order to achieve their objective.

This may involve some level of persuasion, perhaps with incentives or highlighting benefits of a particular path of action. This should not, however, amount to bribery, coercion or cajoling as this would take away from the enabled individual responsibility for their decisions, action and the process of learning. The importance of this type of internal choice is that the learning and change are more likely to be permanent and not conditional on the existence of a reward or threat.

These principles are fundamental to many currently used approaches in safeguarding, including action learning, coaching and solution-focused brief therapy (SFBT). SFBT is the basis for the Signs of Safety model which has been adopted for use in many child protection conferences.

So, based on the above four examples:

- The child may behave in a particular manner because they have decided that this is the right thing to do rather than because of the promise of a reward.

- The carer may end a violent relationship because their child will be safer rather than to avoid legal proceedings.

- The social worker may be more direct and honest because of the benefit to a child rather than fear of a poor appraisal.

- The manager may become more available to practitioners in order to improve outcomes rather than to meet performance targets.

Enabling an individual may also involve assisting them to develop the skill, knowledge, behaviour and environment to enable them to develop the ability and opportunity to take appropriate action. Otherwise, no matter how committed they are to making a change, they may simply not know how to take the first step. Clear guidance and support may be required to address this. For example, a mother who is dependent on alcohol and does not know of available local support agencies may require information and support to develop this knowledge and to engage with these services.

It is normally most helpful for the enabler to present their observations, opinion and analysis as their professional position, which is based on the best available evidence and observation. The basis of their views should be clear and presented in a logical, balanced, consistent and confident manner. However, it can also be acknowledged that this position may be open to challenge, disagreement and the possibility that there may be other valid positions. This recognises that the professional is fallible and, with the best intentions, can misjudge, overlook and misinterpret information. This issue was highlighted by Eileen Munro when she stated that 'the single most important factor in minimising errors is to admit that you may be wrong'.[25] This open and honest approach may enable others to express different or conflicting views, and lead to healthy discussion and exploration which may result in a collectively accepted position. As will be explored later, crucial to effective safeguarding is the development of relationships based on respect, communication and trust. Professionals being open and honest about their own limitations can be very important in promoting these values.

Addressing fear and anxiety

Even with the highest levels of motivation, it is unlikely that interventions will ensure the safety and welfare of children if practitioners or families are constricted by fear, anxiety or lack of confidence. As discussed, stress and pressure are aspects of the safeguarding environment with individuals often feeling overwhelmed and unable to meet demand. This can potentially lead to anxiety, illness, low morale and misjudgements. For example, a social worker may know that they should raise an important issue with a family but may not do so because they fear hostility or violence from a family member.

Similarly, family members may need to overcome fear, anxiety and low confidence in order to address issues which may be affecting the safety and welfare of their children. For example, a mother may need to overcome considerable fear and anxiety in order to address her relationship with an abusive partner before she is able to protect herself and her children.

This is clearly difficult to do and the individual may require considerable courage to address their behaviour and environment. This will be particularly true if linked to deep-seated issues or experiences. Support may be required and it may take considerable skill, time and perseverance to enable the change. For example, the social worker who is frightened or uncertain about how to raise a key issue with a carer may need to be accompanied by a manager or colleague to a meeting with the carer. The social worker may require help with developing new skills or knowledge and an opportunity to practise their approach in order to develop confidence to respond to potential objections and challenges from the carer.

Confidence is defined by Burton and Platts as 'the ability to take on appropriate and effective action in any situation no matter how challenging it is to yourself or others'.[26] This implies that the situation is seen in a clear way and that the individual feels prepared and able to address the worst case scenario. Clarity and focus of purpose are important aspects of confidence as they provide a sense of direction in terms of what to do in any situation. Fear and anxiety are often based on exaggerating or distorting the *likelihood* and *consequences* of an undesired event. In terms of likelihood, this may involve seeing something which *might* occur as if it was *likely* to do so. An example of this would be hypochondriac who considers a symptom as probable evidence of illness rather than being an indicator of a range of possibilities, most of which are not a cause for anxiety. In terms of consequences, this can involve considering the impact of the undesired event as disastrous rather than probably quite manageable – for example, a practitioner who sees the impact of a possible decision as totally destructive when, in reality, it would probably only mean some additional work.

It is important that these exaggerations and distortions, which cause fear and anxiety, do not lead to self-doubt, lack of confidence and avoidance of important issues and tasks. Many of these exaggerations and distortions are unconscious, and it is therefore important to assist the individual to develop awareness of how they may be viewing a situation and develop a balanced and proportionate view of the worst case scenario and likely case scenario. It is important in developing confidence that an individual has strategies and responses to deal with a range of possible outcomes and events. As suggested by Burton and Platts above, confidence is basically a matter of feeling that any situation can be managed. Supervision, counselling, coaching and other development approaches can be used to assist practitioners and families to consider and practise responses to envisaged difficulties and challenges. These approaches can help them develop confidence and explore appropriate ways to raise issues which can reduce the likelihood of undesired outcomes and increase the likelihood of positive outcomes.

Developing the skills and confidence of the workforce

As already considered, many of the training events and publications available to safeguarding professionals have focused on developing knowledge of guidance, procedures and best practice. Some training events have also focused on skill development, for example involving opportunities to practise particular interventions. The effectiveness of training and development programmes can be significantly improved if they also focus on the major motivational drivers relating to safeguarding professionals' purpose, identity and beliefs.

When social workers are asked to identify what motivated them to join the profession, answers very often involve a commitment to ensure children are appropriately cared for and to address social inequalities or unfairness. These are very powerful motivational factors, which clearly link to purpose, identity and beliefs. They need to be reinforced to provide a clear focus in their work with families. Connecting with purpose, identity and beliefs is crucial to ensuring there is a sense of direction which enables skills and confidence to develop. As already discussed, working closely with families enables social workers to develop and maintain their focus on tangible aspects of how children are being unfairly and cruelly treated. This should motivate the practitioner to ensure children's safety and welfare are addressed by the safeguarding intervention, providing a sense of purpose which makes it more likely that practitioner skills, knowledge and behaviour will develop to meet the challenge.

Bringing about change in families

Safeguarding intervention involves a considerable amount of exploration and assessment including gathering information, interviewing family members, liaising with partner agencies, identifying risk factors, analysing and evaluating information, and formulating a plan to address the issues. This process of exploration and assessing and planning is considered to be a cornerstone of safeguarding practice and essential in completing formal assessment documents including assessments and reports for child protection conferences and court.

This can, however, lead to too much focus on the presenting issues and the reasons for safeguarding agencies to be involved. The family can see this as negative and critical and have the effect of demoralising and demotivating them. In addition, it can make it more difficult for the family and safeguarding professionals to work effectively together.

If it is confirmed that a child has been mistreated, then effective intervention must involve ensuring that changes take place within the family and that these result in the child's safety and welfare being positively addressed. This will involve identifying what change is required and how it can be enabled, including highlighting strengths within the family, commitments they are prepared to make and the benefits for change. In order to enable this change, families must be encouraged and supported to reconsider and develop their sense of purpose and identity. In this way fundamental long-term change can take place and there is a significant likelihood that beliefs, skills, behaviour and environmental factors will be addressed in order to ensure the safety and welfare of the child.

The crucial challenge for safeguarding practice is to balance the need to identify risk with the need to focus on change. As mentioned for many practitioners gathering information is considered to be a more established and familiar aspect of safeguarding intervention. Bringing about real and lasting change is always going to be difficult, particularly with family members who have made very deep-seated lifestyle choices. This will be explored further in Step Three.

Pace of change

A final aspect of change relates to the pace at which it is reasonable to expect it to take place. Central to safeguarding practice is the concept that there should be intervention which is undertaken within the child's timescales to prevent the long-term and profound effects of maltreatment or neglect. Emotional stability is important to children and the uncertainty associated with protracted safeguarding interventions can therefore be very detrimental to them. Court processes have recognised this and aim to conclude legal proceedings within six months. It is therefore important that safeguarding interventions are undertaken and concluded within reasonable timeframes, requiring clear focus of planning to address the risk factors to children.

As mentioned, the root problem affecting the safety and welfare of the child almost always relates to the lifestyle, skills and needs of carers. Most commonly these involve substance misuse, mental/emotional health, learning disability and exposing the child to violence or abusive relationships. These deep-seated issues may not be easily resolved. However, it is important to have a timeframe which meets the best interests of children, and achieves reasonable progress. The first six to twelve months is the period of intervention when there is probably the greatest amount of focus and energy and it could be argued that if reasonable evidence of change cannot be observed during this period it is unlikely that it will take place at all.

For example, a mother may engage with an alcohol dependency programme and within six months fail to demonstrate the ability to significantly change her use of alcohol. Whilst about two years would normally be considered necessary to fully address alcohol dependency, it may be reasonable to conclude, within the six months, that there is sufficient evidence to believe that the mother is not able to address her alcohol use. Further support and monitoring would be appropriate, but it is reasonable at this point to consider further legal intervention to ensure the safety and welfare of the children. These measures may lead to the mother realising the consequences of her alcohol dependency, including possibly losing the care of her children, and this may motivate her to find a commitment to address her alcohol use.

Developing healthy and effective relationships

Developing healthy and effective relationships should be seen as important at all levels of the safeguarding environment, particularly between:

- safeguarding managers
- managers and practitioners
- safeguarding agencies
- practitioners
- practitioners and carers
- carers
- carers and their children.

Of course, it is the healthy and effective relationship between carers and their children which is the ultimate focus of safeguarding. All the other levels of relationship can fundamentally be seen as enabling the relationship between carers and their children to develop, which is most likely to happen if the relationships involving professionals and carers reflect the same healthy dynamics. This is an example of 'modelling', which can be very effective in influencing others to adopt desired behaviours.

For example, if agencies are involved with a family due to verbal and physical abuse between carers, the focus of the intervention may be to enable the carers to develop respect for each other and to resolve their differences in an appropriate and non-abusive manner. This approach will be reinforced and have a greater chance of success if practitioners are seen to be respectful of each other and with the family. This will involve developing healthy relationships, communicating effectively, recognising differences and working constructively to resolve disagreements. In turn, this is more likely to happen if practitioners are treated in the same constructive manner by their managers and others within their organisations.

In the emotionally charged environment of safeguarding it is not surprising that the principles of healthy and effective relationships are often forgotten or compromised. There is sometimes a high level of urgency and pressure on professionals and families to react and make decisions without having the time or opportunity to adequately explore issues and consider the full complexities of the situation. Whilst understandable in a crisis situation, this can be very damaging for the relationships and makes it more difficult to achieve positive long-term outcomes. As will be considered, whilst some situations require a crisis response, with most safeguarding situations there is time to respond following exploration and consideration.

The issues considered here are complex and interlinked. It is important that all those involved with the safeguarding of children consider these as crucial aspects of their personal and professional development so that relationships can be positive and productive. It is important that these matters are explored with families and that there are forums to enable professionals to consider factors which affect them. In all relationships it is important that there are opportunities to voice views, observations and suggestions honestly and openly. It may also be necessary for issues to be escalated to an appropriate level of management within safeguarding agencies where these can be highlighted and resolved. As already considered, over recent decades there has been criticism of senior managers as being 'out of touch' with practice. The Ofsted inspection framework, which started in November 2013, has 'leadership and management' as one of its key areas, which includes examining how issues are escalated and resolved.

Value, dignity and respect

Healthy and effective relationships mean that individuals treat each other with value, dignity and respect. This involves building rapport and understanding and is likely to involve considerable attention to courtesy, honesty and empathy.

This is easiest to achieve when individuals act in a manner which is compliant, helpful, competent and appropriate. However, the real challenge, and the proof of healthy and effective relationships, is how issues are responded to when this is not the case – for example, when an individual is being unreasonable, inconsistent, hostile or evasive. Developing healthy and effective relationships involves accepting these behaviours as understandable, especially in challenging situations, and being able to respond to them in a way which constructively engages with the individual. At the root of this is an assumption that individuals are attempting to achieve the overall best outcome and doing so within the limits of their experience and ability.

There may be occasions when an individual is acting in an abusive and destructive manner. This will be addressed in Step Two, but for now it will be presumed that individuals are seeking to develop constructive relationships, albeit within a complex and emotionally challenging environment.

Showing value, dignity and respect is crucial when enabling individuals to listen, debate and respond positively to the matters being discussed. It is within this context that individuals are most likely to engage with and be influenced by others. It also means that differences and conflicts are most likely to be addressed. This is normally most successfully achieved when individuals feel they are able to state their own position and views honestly whilst also being able to listen and understand the position and views of others. Through this, individuals can recognise and value each other whilst challenging assumptions, understanding and conclusions.

Listening and understanding others goes far beyond simply the words being used. It is often said that only 7 per cent of communication relates to the words which are used, with the remaining 93 per cent relating to body language and tonality.[27] This suggests that most communication is unconscious and relates to a wide range of aspects including emotions, current priorities, perceptions and judgement on the part of both speaker and listener. The interpretation of what is being said is also influenced by how the listener perceives the integrity of the speaker, including consideration of contradictions in what is being said, issues which are being evaded and what is motivating them.

Developing trust

Trust is often considered to be one of the most fundamental aspects of a healthy and effective relationship. Two key aspects which relate to trust are the *consistency* and *appropriateness* of behaviour.

- *Consistency* means that it should be reasonably clear what an individual is likely to do or think in a situation. Individuals will be inconsistent, and therefore less trustworthy, if they have mood swings, are unpredictable in their responses or where the reasons for their behaviour are unclear.

- *Appropriateness* means that an individual acts or thinks in a justifiable, clear and reasonable manner. It is not necessary for actions and views to be agreed with but it should be clear that other views and positions have been understood, acknowledged and valued. Individuals will be considered less trustworthy, if the reasons for their behaviour are considered to be unclear, invalid or have not taken proper account of other views and positions.

Developing trustworthiness therefore requires high levels of communication, understanding, openness and honesty. It is important that areas of uncertainty, confusion or conflict are resolved. Consistent and appropriate behaviour create a sense of safety and stability, crucial to a healthy and effective relationship. With a good sense of trust most issues can be resolved, but if there is a lack of trust even relatively small issues can become intractable and damaging.

Acting in a consistent and appropriate manner is often associated with integrity. As already mentioned, this is motivated by an individual's purpose and identity which in turn will influence their beliefs, skills and behaviour. Integrity can also be seen as being like a compass which always points an individual in the correct direction, even when surrounded by conflicting or confusing elements. Early periods in a relationship will often involve *testing out* behaviour when, consciously and unconsciously, an individual's behaviour is observed and considered in terms of whether it is consistent, appropriate and showing evidence of integrity.

As trust involves individuals acting appropriately, it is less likely to exist if there is a lack of skill, confidence and experience. For example, a manager may have difficulty trusting a newly qualified practitioner, or a social worker may have difficulty trusting an inexperienced mother. Skill, confidence and experience are, however, most likely to develop in an environment where dignity and respect are valued and individuals are nurtured and supported to develop ability and understanding. This is challenging as it involves working with individuals who, for at least a period of time, may not respond consistently and appropriately. It is important that recognition, value and respect are given to the skills and abilities which can be trusted and that this is used to develop confidence to explore areas of further development. As already considered, there needs to be a balance between, on one hand, trusting and encouraging independence and self-belief whilst, on the other, having an appropriate level of monitoring to ensure that inexperience or lack of skill does not lead to poor practice or unsafe care of a child. This recognition of strengths and areas of improvement should be the focus of all safeguarding planning and professional appraisal.

Communication

Edwin H. Friedman referred to communication as 'the emotional context in which a message is heard'[28] and is also often highlighted as a key aspect of a healthy and effective relationship. Good communication will both require and promote trust and is closely associated with individuals being treated with value, dignity and respect.

Central to communication is conversation which, put most simply, involves one person making a statement to which a second person makes a response, which in turn leads to the first person responding to the second person and so forth. However, these responses commonly relate to limited aspects of what has previously been stated and therefore involve considerable choice on the part of the responder. In this way conversations are unique and involve a complex process where both participants select and focus on what they feel to be important through how they respond to each other. As Reder, Duncan and Gray stated, 'communication...is a complex process, and integral component of human behaviour and of inter-personal interaction'.[29] The resulting communication can become very open, creative and powerful with new ideas being inspired and created, agreement and common ground being found and areas of disagreement being identified and embraced. Alternatively, the communication can also involve individuals becoming entrenched in their position, ideas being distorted or misrepresented, and disagreement being seen as grounds for hostility. Developing trust, value, dignity and respect are crucial in ensuring that communication leads to positive outcomes and development of healthy and effective relationships.

Rapport is an important aspect of all conversations and communication and is defined by Mo Shapiro as 'the process of building and sustaining a relationship of mutual trust, harmony and understanding'.[30] It is the process by which an individual suspends their own position, views and focus in order to understand the other person's views and perspective. This involves being non-judgemental and respectful of the other person with the genuine intention to learn about them and communicate effectively. In this way, how an individual responds in a conversation is not based on what they see to be important but rather on what appears to be important to the other person.

Listening is an important aspect of this. It exists on many levels, including consideration of:

- words which have been used
- body language and facial expressions
- inferred views, opinions and beliefs
- feelings and the emotional context
- motivation
- what is being avoided or not stated.

The response, in addition to considering these elements, may also consider many aspects including:

- contradictions, inconsistencies or incongruences
- outcomes and what is wanted or sought
- what the listener is wanting to happen
- commitment to resolving issues
- levels of responsibility.

Clearly these are potentially highly complicated dynamics, most of which take place unconsciously, meaning that even very short conversations can quickly become very complex.

Good listening often leads to questions being asked which enable further exploration and can significantly change the direction of the communication. Well-chosen questions, based on careful listening and understanding, are generally considered to be a powerful technique in unlocking issues and enabling significant changes in perspective and understanding. Asking good questions is normally considered to be at the heart of effective counselling and therapy. However, even on a day-to-day level, they can have a significant impact and be much more effective than offering advice or sharing experience.

Difficult or unproductive conversations are often caused by individuals not listening to what is being said and failing to observe the non-verbal behaviour. Instead the 'listener' may be focused on their own views and position. This can often involve them thinking about what they will say next rather than considering what is currently being stated. This can often take the form of interruptions and unhelpful body language, which can be experienced by the other person as disinterest, disrespect or hostility.

Use of emails

Over the last 15 years a considerable amount of communication has been in the form of emails. These are an incredibly useful medium to convey information, for example material, updates and records of meetings. However, it is less likely that sensitive or complex issues can be resolved in this manner. It is common for issues to be discussed through a chain of emails, which may involve a significant number of individuals being copied in, some of whom may then contribute to the exchange. This is a highly ineffective means of communication and very often leads to the matter remaining unresolved or becoming more complicated. It is worth considering whether issues that are not resolved by a single response to an email require a personal conversation, either face to face or by telephone. Following such conversations, an email is often a very helpful means of confirming and recording what has been discussed and any agreements or actions required.

Emails sent to a group of individuals can be considered the equivalent of addressing a meeting. In this scenario there is normally no individual to whom the conversation is directed and no individual who is particularly expected to reply. As with any exchange, it should be clear if an email is being directed to an individual and whether a response is being requested. Copying others into this email is the equivalent of inviting others to observe or listen in on a conversation. This would be unusual in a personal conversation but is very common in email exchanges.

In order to develop an effective safeguarding culture it is important that attention is given to the role and purpose of emails as a means of communication. This should address when the use of emails is preferable to a matter being addressed at a meeting or on a one-to-one level. Also, a considerable amount of time is spent by social workers writing and replying to emails and therefore they represent a significant investment of resources. Consideration should therefore to be given to how they enhance healthy and effective relationships and contribute to meeting the purpose and focus of the organisation.

Resolving conflict

In terms of relationships involving families and safeguarding professionals, it is crucial to consider how conflict and disagreement are addressed and resolved. It is common for those wishing to maintain a comfortable relationship to avoid areas which may cause conflict or disagreement. Such relationships are limited and may not be considered to reflect the principles of healthy and effective relationships. It is important that conflict and disagreement are valued and embraced. The issues relating to these provide an opportunity for individuals to listen to, explore and understand each other's understanding, opinions and patterns of thinking. Conflicts are often a good opportunity to identify and address fundamental aspects of the relationship. For example, a conflict between a carer and social worker may be rooted in the carer's objections to safeguarding agencies' involvement. The resolution of this area of conflict is therefore a useful opportunity to engage the carer through clarifying and focusing on the reasons for safeguarding involvement. Alternatively, the conflict may relate to the style of intervention, so exploring and understanding this may be very helpful in negotiating the most comfortable and effective means by which the social worker can relate to and work with the carer.

In attempting to resolve conflict it is important that there is an honest and open dialogue so that the conflicting positions can be clearly understood. This requires high levels of listening and perseverance to appreciate the reasons for someone holding views which may be very different or based on a different premise. It is worth considering to what extent areas of disagreement are important. There can be a tendency to want to resolve a conflict out of pride or principle when in fact this may not be necessary as the area of conflict may not be particularly relevant or important with regards to the purpose of the relationship.

Consideration may need to be given to whether areas of conflict can be tolerated and accepted. These may relate to reasonable differences of opinion where individuals can 'agree to disagree'. This involves respecting and being tolerant of others' views. However, some views and positions may be considered unacceptable and to agree to disagree would amount to collusion and tolerance of an unacceptable position. For example, a carer or professional may state a view based on a racial stereotype or managing a child's behaviour in a manner considered abusive. These views should be considered as unacceptable and require challenge rather than tolerance. Most situations are, however, less extreme, requiring considerable skill and judgement to decide an appropriate response.

Whilst attempts should be made to resolve issues, it is not necessary for individuals to feel under pressure always to find agreement. Some conflicts can only be resolved through being escalated to a higher authority. This may involve referring the matter to a manager, child protection conference or court. What is important is that the areas of disagreement and the basis of various views on the issue are clearly articulated, acknowledged and understood. When escalating matters the most important aspect is to be clear about what resolution or guidance is being sought.

Directive relationships

Safeguarding intervention sometimes involves managers being very direct with practitioners, or practitioners being very direct with family members. This means a high level of instruction and low level of exploration and discussion. It may be that a practitioner who has a very directive manager will echo this approach with a family member. High levels of directness may be caused by the pressure and requirements on social workers to ensure that actions are being followed and the safety and welfare of children are being addressed.

This direct approach may be appropriate in extreme circumstances. However, it is likely to be unhelpful in developing long-term, healthy and effective relationships. This is also likely to be in opposition to learning, communication and the development of trust, value, dignity and respect.

At a more extreme level, the manager's relationship with practitioners or the practitioner's relationship with the family may become hostile and abusive, perhaps involving specific or implied threats if expectations are not met. This type of relationship can be very damaging and may even involve mirroring aspects of misuse of authority which have led to a child being mistreated. These exchanges can mean that managers and practitioners are considered to be interrogatory, aggressive, over-critical or bullying.

This can lead to the recipient self-blaming, feeling helpless and losing confidence. Fear can mean that they feel unable to confront or address the situation due to the possible consequences. The nature of these relationships is often made more confusing and difficult due to perpetrators at times also displaying positive, caring and appropriate behaviour, which may encourage the recipient to retain some commitment or feelings for them.

In order to address these difficult issues it is important that the safeguarding culture has the facility for individuals to voice their concerns and experiences and for these to be listened to and addressed. It is easy to see why managers may become over-directive of practitioners and why practitioners may be over-directive of families, but it is important that this is seen as an issue which can be addressed, resolved and learnt from.

Styles of authority

For many people the concept of authority is an uncomfortable one, often being associated with abuse of power, autocracy and dictatorship. Many people are motivated to work in safeguarding practice because they want to address inequality and unfairness, and therefore issues relating to the misuse of authority can be particularly sensitive and challenging. However, safeguarding practice is strongly associated with authority and it is important that approaches are developed which promote the use of authority in a positive and appropriate manner.

The use of management styles

The term 'manager' is defined by the Oxford Dictionary as 'a person controlling or administering a business'. The role of a manager is generally seen to include:

- being consistent and reliable
- working within a framework
- focusing on setting objectives
- analysing and making good use of data and information
- ensuring effectiveness and efficiency
- auditing and monitoring performance

- holding others to account
- developing systems and processes
- ensuring financial limits are set and adhered to.

In the 1990s most first line managers in children's social services departments were called team 'leaders'. However, since the mid-1990s the commonly used term has changed to team 'manager'. This suggests a national view that a focus on the management of social work cases will determine the best outcomes.

Stephen R. Covey argues that one of the common and significant difficulties with organisations is their tendency to attempt to *manage* people. He believes that management is appropriate and necessary in relation to *things* such as budgets, stock and buildings, which need to be controlled and handled. However, people do not normally want to be controlled, handled or treated as things. Covey believes that individuals are influenced by a complex mixture of feelings and responses relating to aspects such as their values, beliefs, needs, wants, concerns and worries. If these issues are not taken into consideration then it is unlikely that an individual will take on ideas or perform with energy, effectiveness, efficiency or a good sense of morale.

Covey argues that the traditional model of managing people is based on an authoritarian approach where 'a few people are able to control the rest'. It is closely associated with a belief that people can be motivated through reward and punishment, which Covey refers to as the 'great jackass theory of motivation'. Whilst being the dominant management style over many decades he believes that it is limited, incomplete and can only be partially successful in meeting organisational objectives. This is due to its failure to fully understand and meet the emotional needs and wants of most individuals, leading them to feel 'done to' and micro-managed.[31]

As discussed earlier, in a safeguarding context considerable energy is invested in procedures, guidance and best practice material supported by training programmes to ensure that they are understood and implemented. In addition, performance management and auditing systems are set up to monitor whether the expected actions have been undertaken. All of these can be seen as aspects of a managerial style where the focus is on being clear about what should be done, monitoring that objectives are met and ensuring that resources are utilised effectively and efficiently.

This style of management, based on instruction, control and monitoring, can be referred to as involving *extrinsic motivation*. It attempts to motivate action through direction and requirements which are external to individuals. Such an approach can be effective as long as the pressure is maintained. If there is an alleviation of this pressure, then it is likely that individuals will not maintain the expected practice. Extrinsic motivation is therefore dependent on a reward or punishment being present. In some situations these may be tangible, for example related to a financial bonus. However, in a safeguarding context reward and punishment can be very subtle, for example relating to levels of personal and professional approval.

In a safeguarding environment controlled by extrinsic motivation, it is most likely that individuals will feel they have little influence and not take personal responsibility. They are likely simply to do what is required and be particularly aware of those tasks and actions which are most monitored and considered a high priority. In this way the maxim 'what gets measured, gets done' becomes true, but the tasks and actions may be completed in order to meet requirements for their own sake and not necessarily to ensure the safety and welfare of children. So visits to children may be undertaken to meet requirements but insufficient attention may be paid to their quality and effectiveness in achieving best outcomes.

In addition, a culture based on extrinsic motivation is generally felt to be one in which practitioners and managers are directed and told what to do. Many people will respond by resisting the requirements. This may include doing them in a half-hearted fashion, leaving them until reminded or simply avoiding doing them at all. The individual may make clear undertakings but with little or no intention of following them through. This is often referred to as 'disguised compliance' and is recognised as something which carers will do during safeguarding interventions, as highlighted in many serious case reviews and public inquiries. Less recognised is how disguised compliance is often also used by social workers and safeguarding professionals as a means of avoiding difficult or challenging duties.

The alternative is to consider *intrinsic motivation*. This involves the powerful motivation coming from within an individual and based particularly on their purpose, identity and beliefs. This is a more difficult culture to develop and nurture but there are significant benefits as the quality of work undertaken in this environment is more likely to be motivated by a professional's desire to deliver best practice. With intrinsic motivation, effective safeguarding practice is more likely to be undertaken even if there is no performance requirement, direction or monitoring.

Given the political, public and professional scrutiny on performance, it is clear that practice guidance, procedure and performance monitoring systems will remain in place and that there will always be a significant level of extrinsic motivation in safeguarding practice. As will be explored, developing intrinsic motivation, as an inherent aspect of the safeguarding culture alongside the extrinsic motivators, can lead to significant change in perspective and motivation, resulting in a much more outcome-focused approach.

Three types of problem

To consider further the appropriateness of extrinsic and intrinsic motivation, it is important to examine the nature of the problems which safeguarding practice is attempting to resolve. Based on the work of Rittel and Webber, the following are three types of problem.[32]

- *Simple problems* involve straightforward issues which are commonly encountered and have a well-established operational procedure. The process for managing these problems can often be represented on a flow chart conveying actions required if particular aspects are present. Some safeguarding practice can be considered to address simple problems, for example how new referrals are recorded, providing advice and information, and circulating invitations to a meeting.

- *Critical problems* involve a crisis where there is an immediate threat to the organisation or an individual, requiring decisive and clear action. This is often undertaken in line with procedure and protocol. These problems respond well to direction, with little opportunity for consultation or discussion. A strong management style and extrinsic motivation will work very well with these problems. An extreme example of a critical problem would be a fire alert when everyone needs to be evacuated from a building as quickly as possible. In a safeguarding context, an example would be a child in imminent danger, when action is required to prevent significant harm.

- *Complex problems* involve a number of interdependent or interlocking elements that need to be understood and addressed in combination. The problem may not be clear and may change, evolve and mutate as attempts are made to address it. Indeed, the true nature of the problem may only become clear when it has been resolved. Whilst guidelines may be helpful, the process of addressing complex problems is one of 'feeling your way' and being sensitive and responsive to situations and information as they emerge. Addressing complex problems requires detailed analysis, perseverance, use of various approaches and reflection in order to find the most effective approach to solving the problem. Addressing complex problems can therefore be referred to as both an art and a science. Due to the complexity of these problems there can be no clear operational procedure.

It seems reasonable to conclude that a significant amount of safeguarding practice relates to complex problems. Circumstances causing children to be mistreated and neglected include entrenched lifestyle choices and the needs of carers, which lead to self-neglect, poor confidence, low expectations and emotional trauma. The highly sensitive and emotionally charged environment in which social workers attempt to understand and change these circumstances requires considerable skill, reflection, creativity, flexibility, evaluation, analysis, perseverance and tenacity.

There is often an assumption that safeguarding practice can be addressed through implementing procedure, policy and practice guidance. Clearly, these are important in establishing basic principles, requirements and particular actions which must be considered. They can also provide suggestions, checklists and tools to assist in this process. However, successful engagement is a matter for subtle and skilled human exchange which involves sensitive judgement, astute listening and careful exploration. Only through this can communication, rapport and trust be established which will ensure effective engagement. It is at this level that creative, flexible and reflective practice can be delivered.

This suggests that procedures and guidance, no matter how detailed and clear, will never be sufficient to address the complexity and multifaceted aspects of a significant proportion of safeguarding practice. The Munro Report highlighted the issue of practitioners being unclear about the principles of intervention. They are therefore unable to respond appropriately when the unexpected occurs because there is a lack of understanding about the underlying reasons for policy, procedure and practice.

There is incredible pressure on social workers to ensure the welfare of children and to evidence effective intervention. Political, public and professional accountability all bear heavily on professionals. In this context it is understandable that there will be a wish to control practitioners in the belief that this will improve outcomes for children. This can lead to over-simplified processes and extrinsic motivation, which may be very effective in simple or critical situations, but are unlikely to be effective in complex situations. They may also cause high levels of dependency, anxiety and superficial practice. This can create a vicious circle where the lack of skill, confidence and effective intervention leads to a greater need for managers to be directive, introduce new processes and monitor performance, leading to further loss in skill, confidence and effective intervention. This can particularly be the case when an organisation feels under particular pressure to address its performance, for example following a critical review or Ofsted inspection.

It therefore appears unlikely that a purely managerial approach will be able to deliver effective safeguarding services. It is presumed that practice guidance, procedures, direction and performance monitoring are necessary and must continue to be used in order to meet requirements relating to accountability. What is also needed, however, is the development of an approach which will enhance and complement the managerial approach to ensure the development of professional autonomy and creativity within a framework of best practice. This will involve developing a skilled and confident workforce which will engage effectively with families and partner agencies to ensure the safety and welfare of children.

Leadership

In order to achieve this, practitioners must not only be managed but also be *led*. The Oxford Dictionary defines a leader as 'a person followed by others and who guides by persuasion and example'. Stephen R. Covey differentiates managers and leaders when he states that 'managers work in the system, leaders work on the system'.[33]

There are many definitions of a leader but they are generally seen to include:

- having a clear vision and purpose
- inspiring and motivating
- being inventive and 'thinking outside the box'
- assisting others to make their own decisions
- sharing authority wherever possible
- winning over 'hearts and minds'
- contributing to a constructive and nurturing environment.

Successful leaders will respond to others in a constructive and effective manner which involves trust, value and respect. Within a leadership style the relationship is based on communication and exploration of the issues. A leader is therefore involved in a collaborative approach which aims to think through the situation and enable an agreed outcome based on influence and persuasion. It may be necessary for the leader to give direction or make a decision based on what they feel is required. If the issues have been discussed appropriately then it is more likely that this decision will be seen as reasonable and acceptable.

From the outset it should be acknowledged that a leadership style can initially be more time consuming than a more directive managerial one. At times of pressure it is always tempting to find short cuts and use the most direct route to resolve the immediate issues. Attention may be on survival or simply to get through the current situation. There may not be enough time to have a full discussion and exploration of the issue even if it is accepted that this would be more beneficial in the long term. In these situations it is understandable that a more managerial or directive approach may be used. However, in the longer term this can lead to practitioners not developing their skills and confidence, depending on their managers to offer direction. One of the benefits of a leadership style is that it encourages practitioners to develop greater autonomy and self-reliance based on their skills and confidence.

Of course, most individuals responsible for a group of workers will use a mixture of managerial and leadership styles and there is probably no such thing as a pure manager or a pure leader. The right blend of the two styles means that the workforce benefits from the best aspects of each style as is most appropriate in a given situation. For example, when time is short and the tendency is to be directive, it is normally still possible to take a minute or two to explore and discuss the issues, which can mean that the direction is better understood whilst enabling a practitioner to appreciate the process of thinking through the issues.

Constructive use of authority

The constructive use of authority is a means by which managerial and leadership styles can merge into a cohesive approach. In broad terms, it involves two aspects which need to be balanced. On one hand there is a need to listen, consult, understand and explore issues and on the other is the need to make appropriate decisions, being clear about expectations and actions. If the balance is too much towards the former then the person in authority can be seen as ineffectual and indecisive. If the balance is too much towards the latter then they can be seen as autocratic or dictatorial. Skill and judgement is therefore required to find this balance so that, following reasonable exploration, decisions are most likely to be seen as proportionate and fair.

Within the safeguarding environment there are several key authority relationships, between:

- children and their carers
- social workers and families
- managers and practitioners.

In each of these relationships there is a power differential, meaning that the individual in authority may be required to make decisions on behalf of the other person or insist on them behaving in a particular manner. There is nothing fundamentally wrong with this, but it is important to be sensitive to the dynamics which can result. No authority is absolute and it is important that this power differential is not used abusively, unfairly or disproportionately. There should be clarity about how disagreements can be resolved, and if authority is being used inappropriately what individuals can do. This may involve making a complaint, taking a grievance or raising the issues with a senior manager.

It is worth emphasising that fundamental to each of these three authority relationships is the objective to ensure the safety and welfare of children. Due to the importance of these relationships to safeguarding practice, consideration will be given to each in more detail.

- *Children and their carers*: The constructive use of authority is the basis of a healthy and constructive relationship, with the carer seeking to listen to and understand the views, feelings and position of the child and, through this, to make necessary decisions. The child is then supported and enabled to comply with the decisions of the carer. Most maltreatment of children is rooted in the misuse of authority. With physical, emotional or sexual abuse this relates to how the authority over children is used to serve carers' needs or inflict cruelty on the child. With neglect of children, issues may relate to carers' inability to exercise or understand authority. Carers therefore need to be assisted, through parenting programmes and family support work, to understand the responsibilities which accompany authority and how these can be exercised constructively with their children. When this authority is not being applied fairly, children should understand who to approach, for example a trusted relative, teacher, social worker or national helpline.

- *Social workers and families*: As in the relationship between children and their carers, social workers seek to understand, come to decisions and then support families to comply with these. It is important that the safeguarding environment is developed to enable social workers to participate fully in exercising their authority and for this to be supported by structural systems such as strategy meetings, conferences and legal planning meetings. Recording should reflect the nature of discussion and how decisions were made. In all cases there should be a clear message to carers and children about decisions which have been made and the basis on which this was done. It may involve holding a meeting with the family chaired by a manager. Training for practitioners should include consideration of how authority is used to ensure the safety and welfare of children. When the authority is not being applied fairly, families need to understand who to approach, for example using the agency's complaints procedure or contacting the professional's line manager.

- *Managers and practitioners*: Similarly, the manager seeks to understand, come to decisions and support compliance. Management overview and supervision of practitioners are crucial aspects of effective safeguarding. A key aspect of the manager's role is to monitor practitioners' performance and ensure that they develop the knowledge, skills and experience to undertake their responsibilities effectively. Written appraisals are crucial in identifying areas of strength and development, and ensuring that these are continuously reviewed and updated. As will be explored in Step Two, it is important that practitioners' fears and anxieties are identified to ensure they do not undermine effective practice and that practitioners receive appropriate support. Throughout this supervision, appraisal and monitoring there is a need for the manager to exercise constructive use of authority, and training should enable them to understand and develop the balance between exploring issues and making decisions. When authority is not being applied fairly, practitioners need to understand what to do, for example contacting the manager's manager or using the agency's grievance procedure.

The constructive use of authority involves those in authority making decisions on behalf of others who, even if they don't like the decision, accept the authority and are comfortable with it. Most people have experienced authority being exercised in this positive manner, perhaps by a parent, grandparent, teacher, religious leader or manager. In order to achieve this use of authority it is likely that, in making a decision, the following six elements will be present.

1. There is a base of *value, trust* and *respect*. As discussed, this is the basis of all healthy and effective relationships and is essential in establishing the integrity of the person in authority.

2. *Permission* is given by the recipient. It is easy to think that an individual has authority due to their job title or position. Whilst this may provide a legal or procedural right, on its own this is unlikely to be enough for the recipient to emotionally accept the decision.

3. Issues are *listened to* and understood. There should be a clear sharing of key information, views, observations and preferences. It is important that these are felt to have been fully explored and appreciated.

4. The decision made is considered to be *reasonable* with the benefits and objectives being clearly outlined. This includes the decision being viewed as proportionate, professional, ethical and moral but does not necessarily mean that the decision is agreed with.

5. There is *clarity about disagreement*. It should be clear that consideration has been given to alternative decisions and how weight has been given to different elements in making the decision.

6. *Support* is offered to ensure that the decision is followed through. This means that there is ongoing joint responsibility for the decision and that difficulties experienced in following the decision are considered so that they can be resolved or the decision reconsidered.

This process therefore involves working together to consider the issues, accept a decision and ensure that it is implemented. It is both about the decision made and the process and interrelationship which takes place. This is an important aspect of building trust and respect between both parties.

If any of these elements are not present then there is a chance that the authority and decision will be resented. This may lead to a belief that, as the issues were not properly explored and acknowledged, there is moral permission not to follow the decision. As discussed earlier, this can lead to disguised compliance, with the individual in a position of authority mistakenly believing that decisions have been followed. It is therefore important that all decisions are reviewed to ensure that action has been taken or to consider additional discussion or support which may be required.

Accountability and responsibility

The terms 'accountability' and 'responsibility' are often confused, used interchangeably or considered to have the same meaning. Both terms relate to the actions of individuals and how others see them. However, each has a quite different meaning and understanding this is important in effective safeguarding practice.

- *Accountability* is defined in the Oxford Dictionary as 'the requirement to answer for or provide an explanation for actions'. It therefore relates to an individual's actions, including their motivation and reasons for them. A key forum for considering accountability would be a criminal court, which focuses on accountability for offences and primarily considers what individuals have done or failed to do. In terms of the harm being caused to a child, accountability rests with the perpetrator of the maltreatment and with those who may have encouraged or colluded with it.

- *Responsibility* is a more complex concept as it is commonly used in a number of different ways. First, it is used to imply blame or criticism (as in 'he was responsible for the accident') and in this context it can be confused with accountability. Second, the term is used as a compliment or positive statement (as in 'she acted very responsibly, offering a high level of assistance'). However, it is a third use of the term 'responsibility' which may be most helpful in a safeguarding context. This is to understand it, more literally, as *the ability to respond*.

This definition of responsibility focuses on the choices which can be made in a situation and is in contrast to *reacting* to a situation, which implies that there is no choice. The importance of seeing responsibility as the ability to respond is that, as there are choices to be made, the individual can *own* their decisions and actions. In this context, professional and personal learning can be seen as the process by which individuals consider situations and find more appropriate responses which are consistent with the individual's purpose, identity and beliefs.

Accountability can be seen as relating to what has happened *in the past* and responsibility seen as relating to what may happen in the *present/future*. In a safeguarding context, accountability can be seen as relating to the 'problem', including harm to a child, likely perpetrators, circumstances and root problems – for example, alcohol abuse or mental health problems. On the other hand, responsibility can be seen to relate to the 'solution' and what family members and professionals will do to address current risks to ensure the safety and welfare of children. Balancing focus between accountability (the 'problem') and responsibility (the 'solution') is crucial to ensuring effective intervention. This will be explored in Step Three.

The drama triangle

Transactional analysis has a useful model, referred to as the 'drama triangle', which addresses how individuals distort or avoid facing their own or others' accountability and responsibility. In this model, individuals can act, mainly unconsciously, in three ways in their efforts to apportion an unreasonable level of accountability and responsibility to themselves or others. The three aspects of the drama triangle are as follows.[34]

- *Persecution of others* involves an individual blaming, criticising, scapegoating or being punitive towards others. This means that, rather than attempting to identify and apportion accountability and responsibility in a fair and reasonable manner, the individual seeks to find an easy target. The individual being targeted may have some accountability and responsibility for the situation but these are attributed disproportionately.

- *Being a victim* involves an individual choosing to attack or blame themselves for a situation. Once again, this does not mean that they do not have some level of accountability and responsibility but that they choose to attribute to themselves a disproportionate and unfair amount. This often involves lacking the confidence to consider and express how others may have contributed to a situation.

- *Rescuing others* involves an individual preventing or protecting another person from being accountable and responsible for a situation, often based on a belief that they are unable to cope with this. The consequence is that there is distortion, with accountability and responsibility being disproportionately and unfairly attributed to others.

Fundamental to the drama triangle is that all three aspects are simply different ways of avoiding or distorting accountability and responsibility, relating either to one's own choices or those of another. Individuals are not encouraged or allowed to accept their role in a situation, meaning that effective relationships are unlikely to develop as trust, respect and honesty are likely to be compromised. Emotional needs are also likely not to be adequately met and this can leave individuals feeling frustrated and unfulfilled. As these three roles are fundamentally meeting the same purpose, it is also common for individuals to move between them. For example, someone may persecute others in one situation and see themselves as a victim in another. This may explain why those who have experienced being bullied sometimes also show bullying behaviour.

In addition to these three aspects of how accountability and responsibility can be distorted and misdirected, some individuals will simply avoid or deny any accountability and responsibility for their actions. There may be many reasons for this but most likely it relates to the perceived consequences or being unable to acknowledge their own feelings about what has happened.

Focusing on accountability and responsibility

It is important in safeguarding intervention that issues relating to accountability and responsibility are recognised and incorporated into the work. Considerable courage and emotional strength may be required to focus on and address these issues honestly and openly, and to assist others to consider accountability and responsibility reasonably and proportionately.

The key to this is first to be clear about who is accountable for the maltreatment or neglect of the child. As far as is feasible, this should not be done in a blaming manner but rather in an attempt to be clear and honest about what has happened. It can be very difficult for individuals to accept accountability due to fear of being punished or how they may be seen.

Once there is clarity about accountability it is then important that the response to the situation is considered and that family members and safeguarding professionals accept their responsibility for what is now required to ensure the safety and welfare of the child. This is about moving forward and being solution focused and should be done in a context of acceptance, with valuing of individuals and a belief that, through recognising accountability and responsibility, considerable learning and change can take place.

Clarity of purpose and performance management

Performance management is defined by Pam Jones as 'achieving results through getting the best from people and helping them to achieve their potential…It is an approach to achieving a shared vision of the purpose and aims of the organisation'.[35] This definition is helpful in emphasising that performance management requires clarity of purpose and ensuring that this is met through developing the skills and confidence of the workforce.

Performance management systems were developed in private industry to measure the success of businesses. On a commercial level this can easily be measured in terms of profit and loss. Performance information therefore relates to measurements such as levels of sales, items manufactured, stock held and distribution of merchandise. In this context, the performance measurements are directly related to the company's core purpose of making a profit. As will be explored, ensuring the safety and welfare of children is a more nebulous concept which is difficult to define and measure. This means that it is difficult to identify performance measures which directly link professional activity and analysis to the safety and welfare of children.

The Munro Report focused on how safeguarding agencies give a high priority to performance management, based on national standards and government reporting requirements. The report highlighted how the focus tended to be on quantitative aspects (how often tasks are done) rather than qualitative aspects (how well they are done). Whilst both aspects are important, the lack of focus on the latter was considered by the Munro Report as a significant issue affecting the monitoring of safeguarding practice. The need to move away from predominantly quantitative measurements was summed up by W.B. Cameron first quoted as having stated 'not everything that can be counted counts, and not everything that counts can be counted'.[36]

It is therefore important to consider how quantitative and qualitative aspects of performance can be measured and monitored so that they work together to focus on the effectiveness of agencies to meet the core purpose of ensuring the safety and welfare of children. This issue will be focused on in Step Three.

Developing a clear purpose

At one level, maintaining a focus on ensuring the safety and welfare of children appears to be very simple. However, as suggested earlier, the emotional dynamics inherent in safeguarding practice means that this can be very difficult to achieve. There are many steps and processes involved in meeting this purpose and it is easy for practice to lose its focus and become involved with the process rather than the outcomes for children.

Some of the complexity and challenge of safeguarding practice relate to it being influenced by many factors including children's needs, the quality of care, the role of others involved with children and services being offered. In addition, information about the safety and welfare of children is filtered through the views, perceptions and priorities of many individuals and requires careful understanding, interpretation and evaluation.

There are also many aspects to ensuring the safety and welfare of children. These will be explored in detail in Step Three, but in broad terms they include:

- gathering information about the family
- ensuring that all key agencies are engaged
- developing rapport and relationships with the family and the child
- considering attitudes, lifestyle and the commitment of carers
- recognising protective factors and areas of uncertainty
- identifying risk factors and needs
- analysing and evaluating information and views
- planning for and ensuring change.

These aspects are achieved and monitored through a number of activities and processes including assessments, visits, interviews, professionals' meetings, supervisions and consultations.

Given all of these elements, it is easy to appreciate how social workers may become over-involved in activities and processes and lose sight of the core purpose of ensuring the safety and welfare of children. This is like driving to a destination with many towns along the way. As they are passed through, these places may appear more desirable than the ultimate destination and encourage the traveller to be waylaid. To reach the ultimate destination without undue delay will require a very clear purpose and focus to getting there and seeing the towns as purely points along the route which, whilst interesting, are only a means to an end.

In a safeguarding context, a practitioner may become over-involved in undertaking tasks and activities for their own sake and losing sight of how these can contribute to ensuring the safety and welfare of children. For example they may focus on developing rapport and a good relationship with a carer and view this as of value in itself, rather than in the context of it being necessary to gather information, consider risk and enable change to take place.

The use of quantitative performance monitoring

This tendency to become over-focused on processes is reinforced by performance management systems which concentrate on the timeliness and regularity of activities and processes such as assessments, visits to children and families, supervision, recording, core groups, court deadlines, conferences and reviews.

This can mean that 'what gets measured, get done' and the focus of practice is on improvements in performance management measurements rather than what these are ultimately aiming to achieve. As discussed earlier, at times of stress and pressure, social workers may tend to concentrate on short-term goals and immediate demands, which can lead to focusing on what is being measured.

The difficulty with these quantitative measurements of activities and processes is that they can be diligently and thoroughly undertaken without necessarily contributing significantly to the safety or welfare of children. Assessments can be completed within timescales, cases discussed regularly in supervision and weekly visits undertaken. However, these activities are unlikely to be effective in ensuring the safety and welfare of children unless they are completed with reflection, creativity, sensitivity and with a clear focus on outcomes for children.

Quantitative performance management can also lead to distortions in practice as good results can be achieved by compromising other key practice issues. For example, a good performance measurement can be achieved for the completion of assessments if short cuts are taken and information is not thoroughly explored and analysed. This can mean that the overall quality is low and that the quantitative performance indicator creates a false sense of security about the nature and quality of assessment.

Whilst quantitative measurement can be useful in providing an overall picture of practice, on its own it should not be seen as reliable; it only *indicates* whether practice is ensuring the safety and welfare of children. As suggested, it is the quality of these activities which is also important in judging the effectiveness of safeguarding intervention.

It is understandable that safeguarding agencies, particularly children's services, over-rely on quantitative performance measurement. With the complexity and overwhelming nature of safeguarding practice it is tempting to rely on tangible, simple and easy-to-gather quantitative measures for monitoring practice.

There is, of course, value in quantitative performance measurements. Focusing on ensuring that activities and processes are completed in a regular and timely manner is a reasonable first step in building an effective service. It would be meaningless to discuss the quality of activities and processes if they are not actually taking place. Also, quantitative performance measurement can be used, like a warning light on a car dashboard, to indicate problems which may require further exploration. However, with the extreme pressures on safeguarding agencies it can be tempting to see the information as an end in itself rather than an important contribution to understanding the effectiveness of safeguarding practice.

Over-reliance on quantitative information often leads to a shock when agencies, particularly children's services, are subjected to an Ofsted inspection, serious case review or audit. Whilst these interventions will consider the regularity and timeliness of activities and processes, the key consideration is more likely to be the quality of the intervention and whether this has addressed the safety and welfare of children. Consideration will therefore be given to the quality of performance aspects such as information gathering, relationships with families, multi-agency working, analysis, identification of risk and how outcomes for children have improved. None of these elements are likely to be addressed in sufficient detail as part of a predominantly quantitative performance management system.

The use of qualitative performance monitoring

Monitoring the effectiveness of safeguarding practice, in addition to quantitative performance measurements, requires consideration of the quality of intervention. This will involve a number of approaches, including:

- case audits which examine the quality and focus of activities
- case reviews which consider the approach which has been taken in particular cases
- observations of practitioners and managers
- consultation sessions and surveys with children, carers and family members to find out their experience and perception of intervention
- consultation sessions and surveys with partner agencies.

These methods of qualitatively monitoring practice, whilst very valuable, are also very resource intensive and require professional judgements to be made relating to practice and intervention. This scrutiny can be challenging to social workers as their skills and approaches are exposed and analysed. It is therefore important that there is consultation with practitioners and managers relating to how monitoring will be undertaken and the information used. The process of qualitative monitoring also requires developing a close and sensitive working relationship between professionals involved in a case and those undertaking the monitoring.

It is crucial that this is conducted in a manner which promotes learning and the development of skills and confidence. This is likely to involve good quality feedback and suggestions regarding practice, both in terms of what has been effective and what requires further attention and improvement. These messages and lessons can be very valuable to professionals involved in the case and across the service as a whole. Throughout this qualitative process consideration must always focus on the ultimate performance issue of whether children's safety and welfare is being adequately addressed.

Quality, timescales and resources

In considering performance it is important to consider how quality, timescales and resources work together. All tasks involve these three elements and any change in one of these will most likely impact on the other two. Similarly, if two of these are fixed then the third is likely to be compromised. The way in which these three elements work together is illustrated by two recent high-profile building projects in London. The construction of the London Olympic Stadium required a very rigid *timescale* (to be completed by the opening ceremony) and *quality* (to meet the International Olympic Committee's standards). This meant that the *resources* committed had to be flexible to ensure that these other two elements were met, resulting in the cost significantly exceeding the original budget. In contrast, the contract to build Wembley Stadium defined the *quality* required and the *resources* (or cost) of the project, resulting in the *timescale* being compromised. This meant that the stadium was completed more than two years after the original target date.

In a safeguarding context, if the *resources* which can be deployed to meet a task are fixed and there is a fixed *timescale* for completion then it is likely that the *quality* of the task will be compromised. If this is not acceptable, for example when a crucial court report requires a fixed quality and timescale, extra *resources* may need to be allocated to the task. Alternatively, if *resources* are limited and a high *quality* is required for a task then it is likely that the *timescale* may not be met.

The important point is that all three aspects cannot normally be met, meaning that consideration must be given to which one or two aspects are most important, requiring flexibility and acceptance that performance may not be achieved in the other aspect(s). It is therefore important that there is a sense of realism relating to how these three elements can be met. At times of limited resources and demand for high quality and tight timescales, careful negotiation and flexibility may be required by practitioners and managers to ensure that unreasonable and unsustainable pressure are not experienced by social workers.

The Pareto principle

Developing a clear sense of purpose is reinforced by the Pareto principle, perhaps more commonly known as the '80:20 rule' but also known as the 'law of the vital few' and the 'power efficiency principle'. It was initially developed by the economist Vilfredo Pareto in 1906 and has developed great popularity in a wide range of applications when considering maximising efficiency. Basically, the rule states that 80 per cent of results come from 20 per cent of effort or inversely, 80 per cent of effort will lead to only 20 per cent of results. There are many examples of how the principle has been applied, for example 20 per cent of roads carry 80 per cent of traffic, 20 per cent of the population hold 80 per cent of wealth and 20 per cent of sales calls result in 80 per cent of sales.[37]

The exact 80:20 relationship should be seen as figurative rather than a precise calculation. The principle can therefore more generally be understood in terms of a majority of benefit being gained from a minority of effort. In a safeguarding context an important consideration relates to identifying what actions and tasks are most effective in ensuring the safety and welfare of children. If focus is given to these aspects then the proportionate benefits would be significant.

The principle can also be applied by looking at how a task is performed so that, in the same way, the majority of benefit of each task will come from a minority of the effort. For example, when a social worker receives one hour of supervision, according to the Pareto principle, probably about 10–15 minutes of this will be highly beneficial with the remaining 45–50 minutes having relatively little effect. In addition, with visits to a family, significant benefits can be achieved within a relatively short session. These may relate to checking that there is adequate food available for meals, children's bedrooms are in an appropriate condition or discussing whether a carer attended an important session. This is not to suggest that a supervision sessions or visits should become 'short and sharp' as time will be required to establish rapport. However, it is worth considering how key aspects of meetings can be achieved efficiently, which can reduce the time required whilst increasing focus.

The Pareto principle therefore offers significant opportunities to identify what aspects of actions and tasks lead to the greatest benefit. In this way, at times of reducing resources and increasing demand, clarity of purpose can be developed to maximise those activities which have a significant effect on ensuring the safety and welfare of children.

Summary of Step One

Five things that children's services can do to develop a culture which enables and leads:

1. Undertake a random audit of cases to consider whether safeguarding intervention has led to tangible changes to the safety and welfare of children, focusing on whether the care offered to children has improved, risks are reduced and needs are effectively addressed. If there is no tangible change then the audit should consider what action should be taken, for example reviewing the plan or initiating legal proceedings. If there is evidence of tangible change then consideration should be given to the aspects of the intervention which appear to have contributed to this most.

2. Hold sessions with staff and service users to consider whether the activities of safeguarding agencies enhance learning and change. Key to this is ensuring that creative and reflective thinking is being promoted. This should involve considering how theory and research inform understanding and intervention, the use of feedback and how mistakes, getting stuck and relapses are viewed. Consideration should also be given to how individuals are motivated and enabled to learn and change, giving consideration to how fear, anxiety and other barriers can be overcome.

3. Undertake a confidential survey of staff and service users to explore experiences of their relationships with professionals. This should consider whether individuals feel they have been valued, trusted, respected and treated with dignity. Attention should be given to forms of communication including the use of meetings, letters, telephone contact and emails. Consideration should also be given to experiences of being directed to undertake tasks, how support is offered to enable individuals to come to their own conclusions, the constructive use of authority in decision-making and conflict resolution.

4. Incorporating the outcomes of this survey, hold sessions with all staff to explore how healthy and effective relationships can be developed. Consideration should be given to how management and leadership can be developed and blended to be most effective in addressing simple, critical and complex problems. This should include developing awareness of issues relating to accountability and responsibility, ensuring that this contributes to clarity of planning and understanding the nature of learning and change.

5. Senior managers to consider how quantitative and qualitative information can be gathered and cross-referenced to provide an accurate picture of the effectiveness of safeguarding interventions in terms of improving the safety and welfare of children. It is important that this also considers how performance information can be used to enhance the learning and development of professionals by identifying effective interventions and helping to define clear purpose and focus for the organisation. This should also consider the balance between quality of intervention, timescales and allocation of resources, giving particular attention to specific tasks and activities which appear to be very effective in ensuring the safety and welfare of children.

STEP TWO
Develop a Stable, Skilled and Confident Workforce

Building a stable, skilled and confident workforce is crucial to delivering effective safeguarding practice. As discussed, the delivery of a high-quality service depends significantly on the judgement and actions of practitioners and managers to enable carers to ensure the safety and welfare of children. The workforce also represents the largest financial commitment in most safeguarding agencies so not to fully utilise this represents a significant loss of resources.

In broad terms, a strong, effective workforce will be made up of a stable group of staff whose morale is good and who practise to a high standard. A stable workforce requires a high proportion of staff making a permanent or long-term commitment, meaning that there is a need for successful recruitment and retention. This is strongly influenced by the level of morale and the quality of practice in the organisation as these are normally key to staff and prospective job applicants. In this way there is a virtuous cycle created where organisations with good morale and quality of practice are able to attract and retain staff who further contribute to the positive professional culture.

Being able to attract and retain good quality practitioners and managers is particularly important at a time when safeguarding agencies, particularly children's services, are struggling to recruit and retain permanent staff. Inability to do so can have a profound impact and lead to over-reliance on temporary staff and locum agencies. This can mean transitory relationships between practitioners and their managers and divisive team dynamics. Temporary staff can also have a significant impact on work with families, who may experience more changes of practitioner and lack of continuity in planning. These elements can have an adverse effect on the quality and efficiency of safeguarding services.

In terms of retaining staff, there are many examples of children's services where the stability, morale and quality of practice has been seen as unhealthy and as a result there is a significant exodus of staff and subsequent difficulties attracting applicants for vacancies. This can very easily create a vicious cycle of long-term problems with recruitment and retention difficulties leading to negative effects on stability, morale and quality of practice.

At times of reduced resources most local authorities view safeguarding services as core business and recognise the potential impact on the authority if children's services are unable to adequately ensure the safety and welfare of children. Within this environment credibility is important and this can be advanced if it can be demonstrated that the efficiency and effectiveness of the workforce has been maximised.

Emotional challenges, dilemmas and conflicts

In considering the skills and confidence of social workers it is important to focus on the emotional challenges, dilemmas and conflicts which are inherent in safeguarding practice and examine how these may contribute to difficulties in ensuring the safety and welfare of children.

It is presumed that social workers are committed to doing the best for children and care about those with whom they are working. Therefore, when faced with difficult emotional challenges, dilemmas and conflicts, social workers can become confused, uncertain, distressed, anxious and afraid. This can lead to:

- feeling overwhelmed, demoralised and unable to cope
- being less likely to be creative and reflective
- being more likely to be defensive and process driven
- assessing and developing interventions which do not focus on root problems, risk factors and core issues
- inability to find constructive and workable plans
- developing relationships with families and partner agencies which are over-directive or non-engaging
- being over-accepting of explanations or commitments and failing to be vigilant about risks to children
- having disagreements and conflicts with families and partner agencies which lead to polarisation and poor relationships.

Emotional challenges, dilemmas and conflicts are a significant threat to effective safeguarding practice. It is therefore important that these issues are clearly understood and acknowledged as part of the dynamics of intervention with families. In this way working practices can be developed to ensure that these dynamics do no inhibit effective practice and that practitioners develop appropriate objectives and confidence in meeting these.

The following emotional challenges, dilemmas and conflicts are organised into four groups. These relate to:

- fear and confidence
- relationships with families
- assessing and planning
- balancing demand.

In total, there are 20 emotional challenges, dilemmas and conflicts detailed below. Some of them have already been explored or will be focused on later. They are presented here to enable a picture to emerge about the potential complexity of safeguarding practice and how they can, individually or in combination, contribute to poor or ineffective intervention with families.

Fear and confidence

- *Repulsion at the maltreatment of children*: For the vast majority of people, having children and raising them in a positive manner is one of the highest priorities in life. It is therefore natural for social workers to feel repulsion when in close proximity to those who have mistreated children and may be continuing to do so. This can lead to a range of responses as workers struggle to be balanced and objective. There may be a tendency to punish or blame the carer, leading to potential difficulties in developing a constructive relationship. Alternatively, the social worker may attempt to emotionally avoid the situation by minimising what may have happened or is likely to happen. It is important that consideration is given to these issues when managers are monitoring assessments and plans.

- *Working in an emotionally charged environment*: There are few aspects of life more likely to raise emotions than the suggestion that someone is mistreating their children. Social workers are required to work with carers and family members who are often upset, frightened and outraged by the suggestion. Whether there has been maltreatment of a child or not, the family's response will be highly unpredictable, ranging from passive acceptance to violently challenging the intervention. There may be anger and humiliation about being considered a 'bad carer' and fear that their child may be removed from their care. These issues will be explored further in Step Three.

- *Being honest and direct*: Effective safeguarding practice involves being very honest and direct with carers, family members and partner agencies. This may be in relation to root problems or risk factors, expectations of individuals and their commitment to address issues. The process of being honest and direct is very personally demanding and can be interpreted by others as confrontational and abrasive. Even if delivered in a sensitive manner, there is a reasonable possibility that the response may be hostile, threatening or violent, particularly if an individual does not wish to accept the message. There is also an understandable fear that clearly conveying concern may provoke some individuals to be more abusive to their partner or children. These are important issues to be considered as part of developing practitioners' skills, as will be explored shortly.

- *Fear of putting opinions in writing*: It is common for social workers, when making verbal presentations, to be clear about the root problems or risk factors to a child and how they can be addressed. However, the practitioner can sometimes have difficulty putting this clearly in writing when completing an assessment or report. The reason may be that the views are seen as carrying greater weight when written down and there may be a fear that, if they have misjudged the situation, these views will be referred to for many years. The worker may also fear that a misjudgement could be used as evidence against them in the event of a child being further harmed. It is important therefore that the basis of conclusions is clear, fully discussed with partner agencies and that line managers countersign and share accountability for the conclusions.

Relationships with families

- *Difficulties communicating with and understanding children*: As described earlier, it can be demanding for social workers to develop clear and effective communication with children and this is likely to be even more difficult if the child has been subjected to maltreatment or neglect by a trusted adult. In addition to the trauma and likely mistrust which this may have caused, most children do not wish to cause problems for their family and are therefore naturally less likely to be forthcoming. In addition, social workers are expected to develop a good rapport and relationships with a range of children from infants to adolescents. Each part of this age span requires particular communication skills and it is unlikely that any social worker will be comfortable with and skilled at communicating with children of all ages. These issues will be explored further in Step Three.

- *Offering challenge whilst building rapport*: Social workers are expected to be professionally sceptical, open to all possibilities and not necessarily believe what they are being told. This can be in conflict with the expectation that social workers should maintain rapport, empathy and a good working relationship with families. Too much focus on challenging can lead to family members becoming evasive, defensive or hostile whilst too much focus on building a good relationship can lead to the social worker having a collusive or ineffective relationship with the family. These are important issues to be considered as part of a practitioner's development of skill, as will be explored shortly.

- *Difficulties in gaining a clear picture*: Information available to social workers is often vague, incomplete, unclear, uncertain and unreliable. This is due to many factors including denial or exaggeration of the details, information being speculative or from a third party, contradictions in accounts and information being based on the memories of young children or those with vested interests. Further complexity relates to information being a mix of fact, opinion and supposition. In this context the task of the social worker is very challenging as they are required to process this information, decide what is reliable and use this to form a clear, balanced, evidenced, logical, coherent and defensible picture of the child and their family. These issues will be explored further shortly.

- *Holding a position of authority:* As discussed earlier, for many people authority is an uncomfortable concept however, constructive use of authority is crucial to effective safeguarding. Broadly, it involves two aspects which need to be balanced. On one side there is a need to listen, understand and explore issues and on the other is the need to make decisions and be clear about expectations and actions. If the balance is struck fairly then the latter will most likely be seen as proportionate and fair. There is clearly an imbalance of power in the relationship with the social worker who, on behalf of the local authority, holds considerable authority over the family. It is important for managers constantly to evaluate whether this authority is being used fairly and whether decisions are genuinely in the best interests of the children.

- *Urge to sympathise or think the best of carers:* Whilst being involved in the maltreatment of their child, a carer may also be disadvantaged or a victim of abuse. It can be natural therefore for a social worker to feel sorry for or protective of this carer and be anxious about apportioning accountability and responsibility to them. This anxiety will be greater for social workers who are motivated by wanting to help, support and befriend disadvantaged families. Within this context there can be a tendency to accept an explanation, give the carer the benefit of the doubt or be over-optimistic about their abilities and commitments. This is sometimes referred to as 'hope over experience' or the 'rule of optimism'. These issues should be considered by managers when monitoring assessments and planning.

- *Insufficient time to listen and enable:* An important aspect of developing effective work with families is the ability to listen to and understand their perspectives and experiences. As already discussed, developing healthy and effective relationships and the constructive use of authority require this to take place before a decision is made. Whilst under considerable pressure, time and energy may not be available to undertake this collaborative aspect of the work, meaning that practitioners may be overly directive, leading to insufficient 'buy in' from the family. In this way intervention may be perceived as being 'done to' rather than 'done with' the family. These are important issues to be considered as part of practitioner's development of skill, as will be explored shortly.

- *Balancing the needs of adults and children*: Carers may have been identified as vulnerable individuals due to mental health problems, learning disabilities/difficulties, physical disabilities, illness or dependency on substances. Conflict can arise between how these needs should be met whilst also ensuring the safety and welfare of children. Sometimes this can be evident in the relationships between adults' and children's services, which focus their involvement on the adult and child respectively. Of course, both sets of needs should be addressed and it is important that plans are coordinated to ensure that all vulnerable individuals are treated appropriately and receive the services they require. These issues will be explored further shortly.

- *Telling carers what they must do*: Often the root problem or risk factors which have led to a child being mistreated or neglected relate to a carer's lifestyle, for example, having a violent partner or the misuse of substances. Effective safeguarding practice requires these choices and their effects on children to be highlighted as unacceptable. This therefore involves taking a position which can be seen as intolerant of others or judgemental of the carer's lifestyle and choices. It is understandable that a social worker may struggle with being forthright and direct with carers and consider it an inappropriate invasion. However, it is crucial that social workers are clear that judgement of behaviour is entirely appropriate if this is having an impact on the safety and welfare of a child. These judgements should be voiced as relating to the *behaviour* of an individual and not to the person themselves. These are important issues to be considered as part of practitioners' development of skill, as will be explored shortly.

Assessing and planning

- *Balancing probability*: Once information has been gathered and evaluated, social workers often have to come to a position about what appears to be the most likely explanation relating to the circumstances of a child being harmed. This involves weighing up the evidence and various explanations and, in the 'balance of probability', coming to a conclusion. This is not claiming to be right but rather focuses on what appears to be the most likely explanation, given the available information. There may still be a reasonable level of uncertainty and alternative explanations may be very attractive to others, particularly if these are more comfortable or convenient. Even if the social worker has professionally and thoroughly balanced the evidence, they may still be open to considerable challenge and disagreement from the family and partner agencies. This may be intensified if the social worker's conclusions have significant consequences, for example being crucial to a court application leading to the removal of a child from their carer. These issues will be explored further in Step Three.

- *Being outcome focused whilst being clear about risk*: A key principle of safeguarding is to be outcome focused, meaning that there should be focus on what needs to change and how this will be achieved. This forward thinking is also central to the solution-focused approach which is based on the view that profound change can be brought about through visualising a time when the problem no longer exists. This approach can be in conflict with being clear about the root problem and risk factors. Both these aspects of safeguarding are important and a balance needs to be struck between enabling positive change (solution focused) whilst monitoring the risks to the child (problem focused). These issues will be explored further in Step Three.

- *Finding solutions to difficult problems*: In many safeguarding cases the root problem or risk factors, which have led to a child being mistreated, will be deep-seated and entrenched, for example a carer's mental health, addictive behaviour or emotional difficulties. Addressing these root problems is crucial to the safety and welfare of children, but this may require considerable courage, commitment, insight and motivation on the part of the carer. The result can be that social workers feel trapped between what must change and what is realistically achievable, which can mean they may not sufficiently emphasise the importance of addressing the root problem or risk factor. These issues will be explored further in Step Three.

Balancing demand

- *Maintaining relationships with both the family and partner agencies*: Given the complex nature of safeguarding intervention and the range of perspectives which the family and partner agencies may have, it can be challenging to be seen as fully incorporating and respecting all these positions. The role of social workers is often to adopt a position about the most likely explanation and how this should be addressed. This can alienate either family members or partner agencies who may have a different view. These are important issues to be considered as part of practitioner's development of skill, as will be explored shortly.

- *Quality of intervention and timescales*: As discussed earlier, the quality of intervention is what determines the effectiveness of safeguarding practice. In an attempt to raise standards over recent years, timescales have been introduced which are expected to be met in a high proportion of cases. There can be a conflict between completing work on time and getting it done to an appropriate standard. There is a danger that in meeting timescales important aspects may be avoided. Meeting timescales and the quality of work are not of course mutually exclusive, the time taken to complete a task being an important aspect of quality. It is important for social workers to be aware of the need to maintain a reasonable level of quality whilst being mindful of the timescales.

- *Nature of managerial direction*: It is expected that all social workers will receive regular supervision and guidance on how to progress cases. As already considered, this may involve being over-directive, which can undermine the confidence and development of social workers. It is important that they are given sufficient autonomy, appropriate to their skills and experience, so that the level of direction and guidance informs and supports the worker but does not restrict effective practice or creative and reflective thinking.

- *Balancing the needs of a range of cases*: It is common for social workers to have a caseload which is higher than recommended (15 cases if qualified for over a year) and for the caseload to include complex cases. As a result, most social workers are significantly challenged by the demands of their cases and this often involves balancing demands. This is often done on the basis of those cases which are 'shouting the loudest' and it is important that this is not allowed to mean that other high-risk situations do not receive appropriate attention. The work pressure can also mean that new concerns or referrals are not responded to appropriately, with a risk of them being marginalised or ignored. It is important that these issues are considered as part of the supervision of practitioners.

- *Managing urgent situations whilst maintaining relationships:* There is often a high level of urgency, which means that social workers can be required to make decisions without having the time or opportunity to reflect on the issues and to adequately explore issues with the family and partner agencies. Whilst understandable in a crisis situation, this can be very damaging for the relationship and makes it more difficult to achieve positive longer-term outcomes. Consideration should therefore always be given to the urgency of a situation and whether it may be appropriate to respond in a timescale which allows some involvement with the family and partner agencies.

The impact of emotional challenges, dilemmas and conflicts

On first examination, this list of emotional challenges, dilemmas and conflicts may make depressing reading and provoke the question of why anyone would choose to be a social worker. It is hoped, however, that by detailing these issues, the causes of stress and anxiety can be better understood and managed. All of the issues above are complex and there is no easy answer to them. In many situations the social worker may not be consciously aware of how these are influencing their behaviour and practice. The professional response is to develop awareness and sensitivity to them and vigilance about how and when they may be having an impact on effective intervention.

These elements can have a profound impact on the skills and confidence of practitioners to ensure the safety and welfare of children. Whilst social workers may be clear about what they believe they should be achieving, these elements can make it very difficult, on a day-to-day basis, to keep a clear focus. This can lead to social workers being 'process driven', committing considerable energy and resources without significant benefit to the safety and welfare of children.

These elements can have massive implications for the amount and nature of support being offered to practitioners. High levels of support and challenge are important, and social workers need to develop skills, techniques and strategies to overcome these emotional challenges, dilemmas and conflicts. As highlighted in the Munro Report, we cannot eradicate the 'uncertainty, risk and complexity' associated with safeguarding work. However, it is feasible to develop more effective practice through having greater clarity about the dynamics and factors which impact on the role of social workers and safeguarding professionals.

Supporting and developing practitioners

In supporting and developing practitioners, it is important that skills and confidence are developed which address the emotional challenges, dilemmas and conflicts. The overall aim is to ensure that social workers, in conjunction with partner agencies, meet the requirements of an effective working environment as outlined at the conclusion to the section on Background and Current Environment.

At times of low morale, professionals can focus too strongly on practice difficulties, concentrating on how and why best practice cannot be achieved. This can be demoralising, undermining learning and change. Considerable support and encouragement may be required to enable professionals to move beyond this to understand the nature of the barriers, positively seeking new working practices and ways to overcome difficulties. This process of balancing an understanding of the 'problem' with a focus on the 'solution' is crucial to achieving learning and change. As will be explored in Step Three, this is very similar to the process of bringing about learning and change in families. This also requires understanding the 'problem', for example how children have or may be mistreated, but balancing it with understanding the 'solution', for example how root problems and risk factors will be reduced.

The following are the key ways in which social workers can be developed.

Formal and informal supervision

Supervision involves a mixture of the following four functions:

- *Management of work* including ensuring that policies and procedures are followed, work is progressing satisfactorily and that there is reasonable focus and purpose in the work

- *Learning and development* including providing feedback, undertaking appraisals, identifying learning goals and ensuring performance development

- *Support* including addressing the emotional impact of the work and ensuring that appropriate support and guidance are offered

- *Partnership and joint working* including addressing issues relating to multi-agency working and to other parts of the service.

Given the high demand and pressure of the work, it is often very difficult for managers to offer the levels of support and development which many social workers require to effectively safeguard children.

Formal supervision is a central aspect of managing safeguarding cases and this is ideally considered to be for 1.5 hours every 4 weeks. Even at this level of supervision and with most social workers holding caseloads of 15 children, each child will only be discussed for about 6 minutes every 4 weeks. Clearly this does not allow for anything other than a very cursory discussion. This limited time means that managers are often directive with social workers, which means that they are not enabled or supported to find their own solutions and develop their skills and confidence. Whilst formal supervision is important, it is clear that this cannot be relied on to ensure that there is adequate purpose and direction in all cases.

Social workers normally require a considerable amount of informal advice from their managers. It is estimated that 60–70 per cent of a manager's time can be spent offering support to social workers, most of which is outside formal supervision. The difficulty with these discussions is that they can be rushed, with insufficient time to explore complex issues. In addition, these discussions are often not recorded and issues are therefore less likely to be part of the continuity of planning.

Potentially, an important aspect of the manager's role is to offer day-to-day support to practitioners in terms of accompanying them to court, meetings, visits and other key events. Whilst many managers make themselves available to do this, being responsible for up to seven practitioners means that managers' time is very limited to offer this kind of support. In order to address this, many children's services have created assistant team managers or senior practitioners to provide additional support to practitioners. However, given the pressure to allocate cases, it can be difficult to ensure that these positions are sufficiently free of case holding to enable them to support practitioners.

A further important aspect of supervision is the allocation of appropriate cases to practitioners so that appropriate skills and confidence can be developed. This should be in line with the appraisal of a practitioner's skills as outlined below.

Coaching

Coaching aims to assist social workers to find their own answers to issues and set their own learning aims based on the belief that individuals have the skills and ability within themselves to find solutions. Coaching therefore focuses on drawing this out and offering a space for creative and reflective thinking, enabling participants to explore issues and identify barriers to both professional development and progress on cases. It can also be important in addressing issues relating to work pressure, stress, morale and general well-being. The coaching relationship involves increasing awareness of when a practitioner has successfully managed difficulties and using this to create and build confidence, recognise their own skills and help them find solutions to issues with which they are presented. In this way skills and confidence can be developed.

As change involves exploring different levels of motivation, coaching can be very useful in exploring deeper issues which influence individuals, particularly relating to the more fundamental aspects of purpose, identity and beliefs.

Skills and confidence are most likely to flourish in an environment which supports and expects questions to be asked, assumptions probed, beliefs challenged and strategies developed for working effectively with families and partner agencies. This process of developing insight and bringing about change is similar to how practitioners can effectively work with families, so the coaching relationship should model what is expected of practitioners in terms of their interventions. Coaching should have clear ground rules about confidentially and in what circumstances the coach would share the content of the session with another individual or manager. This would normally be if there was a concern about the welfare of a child, vulnerable person or member of staff.

Coaching is normally offered in either individual or group sessions. The coach requires particular skills, which can be fulfilled by a manager, colleague or external individual. It can be offered as a basic aspect of the development of all practitioners or managers or be focused on specific issues, perhaps in relation to an individual's development plan. This may be part of the informal or formal stages under capability procedures and may focus on addressing specific practice issues.

Group coaching normally involves about six to eight practitioners. The frequency and length of sessions can vary, but typically they are fortnightly and last for two hours. The timescales for coaching can vary from normally a minimum of six sessions to a longer-term basis, as part of a training and development programme. Whilst all coaching will encourage specific examples to be brought to the sessions, in group coaching these examples should be relevant to the whole group.

Coaching must be seen as clearly different from supervision, which concentrates on the four areas outlined above. In this relationship the supervisor is responsible for the quality of the discussion and therefore may not be able to adopt the non-directive and neutral role of a coach. However, some techniques common in coaching, for example enabling supervisees to define their own ideas and suggestions, may be incorporated into the supervision relationship to enhance exploration and learning approaches.

Coaching needs to fully respect and support the role of team managers and senior managers who hold the statutory responsibility for cases. Where coaching supports a social worker to develop ideas about how to progress a case, they may need to discuss these with their team manager, particularly if they involve a change of plan or focus.

Observations

A natural extension of the coaching and supervision roles is to observe social workers on visits or at meetings in order to offer feedback on their performance and to use this to explore ways in which skills and confidence can be developed. This can also provide valuable material for the coaching sessions to explore. With the permission of the service user, video or audio can be used to record the session with the family for training purposes.

It is important to be aware that many practitioners may demonstrate skills and approaches during an observation which they may not normally display. This best behaviour is a strong indicator of what they are capable of doing but may provide a false sense of security if it is presumed that this reflects the usual level of practice. Any conclusions drawn from observations should therefore be confirmed using other sources of information, for example case auditing.

Practice guidance and training workshops

Training has been central to professional development for many decades, focusing mainly on providing information on legal frameworks, procedures, guidance and best practice. This approach to training appears to be based on an assumption that improving practice means addressing the knowledge of professionals. As already discussed, knowledge is an aspect of motivation but more important are purpose, identity, belief and skill. Very often social workers have knowledge of what is expected of them but the real issue is why and how this is incorporated into practice.

In this respect it is essential for practice guidance and training workshops to address the barriers to delivering best practice and identify strategies to overcome them. In this way training events can focus on the skills, confidence and commitment of practitioners to implement procedures, research, theory and best practice. Training events can be very effective when arranged as part of a team meeting. In this way a group of practitioners, with their manager, can consider how they can support and challenge each other to develop a learning culture. These events are an opportunity for safeguarding professionals to work together to identify issues, stimulate new ideas and support each other to address them.

It is important that all practice guidance and training events consider:

- emotional challenges, dilemmas and conflicts, including those identified above
- the nature of bringing about change and what may be acting as a barrier to this
- how creative and reflective thinking can be developed
- how theory and research can inform effective practice
- how interventions with families make a significant difference to the safety and welfare of children.

Consultation on cases

Consultation on cases is common when there is significant complexity, risk or lack of progress. The purpose of the consultation is to identify barriers to progress and strategies for addressing these. Consultation is most often with the social worker and their manager but it can often be helpful to have a wider meeting which also includes the family and partner agency. It is important for agencies to consider the criteria for when consultation should be held. Working with a family ineffectively can be a massive drain on resources whilst still not addressing the safety and welfare of children. Holding an early consultation meeting can therefore be a very good use of everyone's time.

Some children's services review cases when it appears likely that a child is going to be the subject of a child protection plan for over two years, which normally relates to addressing the government performance indicator. It may be reasonable, however, to consider reviewing any child who has been the subject of a plan for over nine months (following a second review conference) if there is no clear evidence of reasonable reduction in risks to the child. As already discussed, if change is not identified within this initial intensive period it may be unlikely to be achieved without a reconsideration of the plan. Holding a consultation session at this stage can add significant clarity and purpose to the work on the case. This consultation session is an opportunity to consider whether a legal planning meeting is required to consider action under the Public

Law Outline or to ensure clear expectations relating to change and the timescale for this.

Child protection conferences also undertake this role, but pressures on them can make this difficult, even if the core group and key professionals clearly report to the conference about attempts to make progress, probable reasons for these being ineffective and proposals for future intervention. With most conferences scheduled six months in advance, they do not normally have much flexibility to ensure there is extra time allowed to meet specific demands of a case and to fully explore complex aspects.

Auditing of cases

As already discussed, auditing is most often seen as a means of monitoring practice performance and compliance within qualitative and quantitative parameters and can be experienced by practitioners and managers as challenging practice. Given the considerable resources and the potential benefits, it is important that careful consideration is given to how audits can be used as a learning tool to offer support, practice feedback and explore the effectiveness of interventions. Audits can also be valuable in identifying more strategic issues which may be affecting a number of cases and to explore ways in which systems and processes can be developed.

Joint working

Joint working can be a very helpful approach with demanding and challenging cases, ensuring practitioners do not lose their sense of purpose. For example, with evasive or hostile family members, it is more likely that joint working practitioners will be able to find strategies to engage and enable an effective intervention. Joint working is like two mountaineers climbing a difficult mountain. If they are connected by a rope there is a reasonable chance that if one slips the other can prevent serious harm. In a safeguarding context, if a worker is being drawn away from the key issues of the case the other worker can redirect the focus back onto these issues. As already discussed, fear and anxiety can prevent practitioners from addressing difficult issues with families and partner agencies but joint working can enable these to be explored, offering opportunities to persevere with helpful approaches, take up complementary roles and reflect on whether further action is required. Whilst resource intensive, joint working can be justified in terms of how it enables practitioners to collaborate to develop practice, share skills and ensure effective intervention with a family.

Self-learning

Study and self-learning are often overlooked as important ways for practitioners to develop their skills and confidence. Computer-based learning is particularly effective for knowledge-based training, enabling individuals to learn flexibly and at their own speed. In addition, the increasing use of webinars or internet-based live seminars allows debate to take place to enable interactive learning. Some self-learning, for example with books and publications, can also be effective in enabling professionals to explore their motivation in terms of purpose, identity and beliefs.

Complaints, comments and compliments

Complaints, comments and compliments represent valuable feedback from service users and partner agencies about how a service has been experienced. These include the three stages of complaints: applications to the ombudsman, issues raised by elected members and informal feedback. Consideration should therefore be given to how these can be used to highlight and explore practice issues and develop more effective interventions. It can be very reassuring to the individual who has raised the issue to know that the complaint, comment or compliment has been listened to and will be used to improve the service.

Supervision and coaching for managers

The role of managers in safeguarding is crucial in ensuring that there is an overview of cases and that planning is effective in addressing the safety and welfare of children. This includes monitoring whether legal requirements, policy, procedures and guidance are being followed.

Supervision and coaching sessions for managers can be very effective in helping them to develop their skills and approaches to monitoring and enable effective practice. As we have seen, the dynamics and challenges in safeguarding practice are very complex and it is important that managers are sensitive to these whilst also ensuring that the agency's core priorities are met. In particular, this will involve developing the stability, skills and confidence of their teams and regularly undertaking appraisals to ensure that capabilities are acknowledged and areas of development are identified.

Practitioner capabilities

The most fundamental aspects of capability to practice should be considered as part of the recruitment and selection process. In terms of social workers, these include confirmation that the practitioner:

- is registered with the Health and Care Professions Council (HCPC)
- has the right to work in the United Kingdom
- has a recent and satisfactory Disclosure and Barring Service (DBS) application
- has satisfactory references, which cover at least the previous five-year period
- is physically and emotionally able to undertake the duties of the post.

Periodically checking that these requirements continue to be met is important in ensuring that the workforce meets legal and procedural requirements.

The HCPC requires that all registered social worker professionals must:

- act in the best interests of service users
- respect the confidentiality of service users
- keep high standards of personal conduct
- provide any important information about conduct and competence
- keep professional knowledge and skills up to date
- act within the limits of their knowledge, skills and, if necessary, refer the matter to another practitioner
- communicate properly and effectively with service users and other practitioners
- effectively supervise tasks that they have asked others to carry out
- get informed consent to provide care or services (except in an emergency)
- keep accurate records
- deal fairly and safely with the risks of infection
- limit work or stop practising if performance or judgement is affected by their health

- behave with honesty and integrity and make sure that behaviour does not damage the public's confidence in them or their profession
- make sure that any advertising is accurate.[38]

Meeting these duties is a requirement for registration for all social workers in England and therefore a legal requirement to practise. They are described by Anna van der Gaag (HCPC Chair) as the 'professional and public expectations of the behaviour' of those registered as social workers, including managers, and should therefore be seen as the most basic definition of the ethical position of social workers.[39]

With the establishment of the HCPC in 2012, there is a requirement for all registered social workers to provide continuing professional development profiles. These profiles are required from registered social workers every three years and there is random monitoring of 2.5 per cent of registrants each year. Failure to submit a record which meets the HCPC standards will result in registration being withdrawn, meaning that it would be unlawful for that practitioner to be employed as a social worker or in any post requiring the professional qualification. Whilst employing agencies have an important role in supporting development profiles, the ultimate responsibility for demonstrating continuing professional development rests with the registered practitioner.

Legal and procedural knowledge

Social workers and managers are required to have a thorough knowledge of key aspects of safeguarding practice, including:

- legislation, regulations, guidance, procedures and protocols
- theory and research
- local and national resources
- eligibility criteria/thresholds for services and how referrals are made
- structure and function of children's services, other local authority departments and partner agencies.

Development of these areas of knowledge can be achieved through a range of approaches, as outlined above. However, training workshops, with dissemination of written information, are likely to be particularly useful.

Skills and qualities of social workers

Crucial to the delivery of effective safeguarding practice is ensuring that social workers have the necessary skills. As discussed earlier, developing them effectively requires practitioners and managers nurturing their purpose, identity and beliefs. It is therefore essential that skills are not viewed in isolation but rather in the context of motivation.

The College of Social Work and Social Work Reform Board have identified the following nine professional capabilities which outline the skills and qualities of social workers. These aim to establish a national framework for vision, capabilities and continuing professional development. The nine items in the Professional Capabilities Framework are:

1. *Professionalism:* Identify and behave as a professional social worker, committed to professional development.

2. *Values and ethics:* Apply social work ethical principles and values to guide professional practice.

3. *Diversity:* Recognise diversity and apply anti-discriminatory and anti-oppressive principles in practice.

4. *Rights, justice and economic well-being:* Advance human rights and promote social justice and economic well-being.

5. *Knowledge:* Apply knowledge of social sciences, law and social work practice theory.

6. *Critical reflection and analysis:* Apply critical reflection and analysis to inform and provide a rationale for professional decision-making.

7. *Intervention and skills:* Use judgement and authority to intervene with individuals, families and communities to promote independence, provide support and prevent harm, neglect and abuse.

8. *Contexts and organisations:* Engage with, inform and adapt to changing contexts that shape practice. Operate effectively within own organisational frameworks and contribute to the development of services and organisations. Operate effectively within multi-agency and inter-professional partnerships and settings.

9. *Professional leadership:* Take responsibility for the professional learning and development of others through supervision,

mentoring, assessing, research, teaching, leadership and management.[40]

Whilst these address the broad intentions of safeguarding, there is insufficient detail to address key issues, relating to effective practice, which are required if agencies are to ensure the safety and welfare of children. For example, the nine capabilities do not highlight skills relating to assessing, recording or planning. They also do not explore the crucial aspects of developing resilience and confidence which are important in meeting the emotional challenges, dilemmas and conflicts inherent in safeguarding practice. It is therefore suggested that this model can usefully be expanded by subdividing two of the capability areas.

First, *intervention and skills* can be seen to include:

- developing healthy and effective relationships
- assessing
- ensuring planning for children
- ensuring progress on the plan.

Second, *context and organisation* can be seen to include:

- maintaining a customer focus
- working within children's services and with partner agencies
- recording and reporting
- developing confidence and resilience.

In this way the nine professional capabilities can address 15 skill areas relating to effective safeguarding practice. Appendix B contains a checklist against each of these 15 skill areas, which can be used to appraise social workers. When planning for an appraisal it can often be difficult to identify issues relating to social workers, both in terms of their skills and areas requiring development. The checklist is therefore intended to encourage creative and reflective thinking, triggering thoughts and recollections relating to practitioners' performance and perspective. Managers and social workers can use the checklist to prepare for the appraisal, enabling each to identify areas which should be acknowledged or explored. In addition, it may also be useful for a third person to assist in the preparation by using the checklist to identify issues and offer views and feedback regarding the social worker.

The focus of appraisals is to ensure continuous improvement across the workforce by first identifying an individual's skills and areas of development. These appraisals can then be aggregated to give an overall picture of the skills and areas of development in the workforce. This will provide a focus for training and development programmes, consider broad organisational issues and influence recruitment initiatives.

Individual social worker appraisals should formally take place on an annual basis with regular reviews throughout the year. When completing the appraisal, the manager should record how the practitioner is performing against each of the 15 skill areas. These should be assessed as meeting one of the following four levels:

- *Outstanding*: The skill area is of a very high standard with no more than minor areas of development required.

- *Good*: The skill area is of a high standard, but with areas of further development required.

- *Requires improvement*: The skill area does not reach the expected standard. However, the social worker is aware of how they can develop and is able and willing to work on this. This area of improvement should be closely monitored and reviewed.

- *Inadequate*: The skill area does not reach an acceptable standard and there is a low prospect that the worker can or will address this, for example due to persistent under-performing. Consideration should be given to using capability procedures to address the performance issues.

In addition to appraisals, it is also suggested that these 15 skill areas are used for recruitment and selection purposes to ensure that those entering the workforce demonstrate appropriate levels of skill. Attention may be given to recruiting practitioners who are particularly skilled in areas which are generally under-represented in the service.

Manager capability

It is presumed that managers will be able to demonstrate all of the 15 social worker skill areas as outlined above. In addition, team managers should be able to demonstrate the following eight areas of skill:

1. developing and managing the team

2. supervision

3. developing staff and monitoring performance

4. ensuring progress and quality intervention on cases

5. allocating cases

6. recruitment

7. responding to complaints and feedback

8. working with partner agencies.

Appendix B provides a detailed breakdown of these eight areas. It is suggested that these should be included in appraisals of managers and used in a similar manner as that outlined above with respect to social workers.

Ensuring the safety of practitioners

Safeguarding intervention is challenging and emotive and will, on occasions, result in challenging behaviour on the part of family members who may find it difficult to discuss the care, safety and welfare of their children. Some of these responses, whilst challenging, may be considered natural and understandable, including:

- displaying fear, anger, agitation, distress, anxiety or worry
- speaking in a raised volume or intense tone
- displaying strong views and emotions
- appearing intransigent or unreasonable
- disagreeing with the practitioner.

It is a crucial part of a practitioner's skill to be able to manage these types of challenging behaviour constructively. An effective relationship between the family and social workers must involve the ability to listen to views and feelings which may be stated in very direct and strong terms.

On occasions, however, the response from a family member may be *unacceptable* and require a more robust response. Examples of such behaviour include:

- *verbal abuse* including verbal attack and shouting or swearing at a practitioner
- *verbal threats* including stating an intent to assault the practitioner or force them to leave
- *discriminatory abuse* including making comments or being dismissive of the practitioner's race, religion, ethnic background, disability or lifestyle choices

- *intimidation* including acting in a manner intended to cause fear in the practitioner
- *threatening behaviour* including relating to the practitioner in a hostile manner
- *sexualised behaviour* including making advances or contact of a sexual nature
- *actual assault* including any physical contact, including use of a weapon, with a hostile intent
- *assault by proxy* including allowing or directing an animal or person to attack or abuse a practitioner.

Practitioners must be supported from the impact of these types of negative, hostile and potentially dangerous responses and behaviour from families. This relates to the employer's 'duty of care' and responsibility to act reasonably to protect the safety and welfare of all staff. Experiencing such abuse can be very upsetting and traumatising for practitioners and can lead to long-term issues relating to morale, confidence and well-being. Personal injury claims are becoming more common and in such cases it is important that employers can demonstrate how practitioners have been assisted in avoiding and managing stress, trauma and injury.

In addition, these unacceptable behaviours can affect the role of social workers in ensuring the safety and welfare of the children. The basis of healthy and effective relationships is seriously challenged by such behaviour and this can make it very difficult for practitioners to make judgements based on balanced and proportionate consideration of information, observations and professional opinion. There is a danger that practitioners may feel intimidated, leading to their over-readily accepting families' explanations or being reluctant to challenge and raise difficult issues. Alternatively, practitioners may react by being punitive, disproportionate or over-reactive. With any of these responses there is a likelihood of inappropriate or unhelpful interventions.

With some incidents there may be disagreement between the family member and practitioner as to whether the behaviour is unacceptable. For example, behaviour may be perceived by the practitioner as threatening but the family member may claim that this was not their intention. This will require careful reflection and consideration by the practitioner and their managers, giving consideration to the safety and welfare of both practitioners and children.

Reducing the likelihood of unacceptable behaviour

It is important that practitioners consider preparatory and precautionary steps which may reduce the likelihood of unacceptable behaviour or its reoccurrence. It is important to emphasise that the accountability for unacceptable behaviour rests with the individual exhibiting it and that this should not be excused or minimised due to actions or lack of preparation by the practitioner. It is, however, clear that certain approaches will enable practitioners to be in a more confident and flexible position which will enable them to manage the family's responses in a manner which is less likely to escalate to unacceptable behaviour. Central to this is the quality of the relationship with the family, including developing an honest and direct approach, having clear expectations, being solution focused and the constructive use of authority. Appendix C contains further information about steps which practitioners can take to enable an effective relationship with families to enhance the working relationship and reduce the likelihood of an incident of unacceptable behaviour.

Personal safety is improved by carrying an alarm or mobile phone with colleagues' and managers' direct lines or mobile numbers pre-programmed for easy access. It is also important that there are robust procedures for ensuring safety during a meeting or visit to a family. For example, when a visit is planned, colleagues should always know where the meeting is and the time the practitioner is expected to return to the office. Visits at the end of the working day, when the practitioner is expecting to go home immediately afterwards, need to be managed carefully and should involve the practitioner phoning a manager or colleague when the meeting is completed.

When assessing the level of risk to practitioners, consideration should be given to all those who live in or visit the household. The strongest indicators of risk to practitioners relate to incidents, recent or historic, which have happened or are believed to have happened. When gathering information on a family, consideration should be given to:

- previous incidents of unacceptable behaviour
- the nature of the present relationship within the family and with professionals
- use of drugs, alcohol or other substances
- mental health issues
- levels of distress or anxiety
- areas of conflict with children's services or other agencies

- potential conflict which may arise due to the purpose of the meeting and likely discussion.

Appendix C contains further information about arrangements which can be made before any meeting, particularly when an individual has demonstrated unacceptable behaviour or where there appear to be grounds to believe that there is a likelihood of an incident occurring.

Response to unacceptable behaviour

In most situations, unacceptable behaviour does not come out of the blue, with most violent incidents being preceded by verbal abuse and threats. It is for this reason that relatively minor examples of unacceptable behaviour should receive an appropriate response in order to reduce the likelihood of more serious incidents occurring.

In all situations where unacceptable behaviour is experienced, the first priority of the practitioner should be their own safety. In situations where there is a physical attack, minimum force should be used to enable the practitioner to immediately leave the situation. There is no need to explain why they are leaving as this can be done later. It may be necessary for the practitioner to leave without some of their possessions. If a colleague or member of the family continues to be in danger then the police should be contacted immediately.

Appendix C contains further information about what action can be considered by a manager following an incident of unacceptable behaviour.

Developing relationships with partner agencies

For many decades it has been a standard safeguarding approach to bring together practitioners from a range of agencies to take collective responsibility for the safeguarding of children. This is coordinated by local safeguarding children boards, which are required across England and Wales. Strategy meetings, child protection conferences and core groups have been developed to ensure all agencies contribute, understand each other's roles and work effectively together, ensuring there is a clear multi-agency analysis of the family so that planning ensures the safety and welfare of children. The assumption is that working closely together will create an approach which is better than the sum of the parts.

Many serious case reviews and enquiries have highlighted safeguarding professionals not adequately communicating, meaning that key information is not shared. This leads to each agency having a partial understanding of the family but there being no overall appreciation of the family's circumstances and the risks to the children. Agencies acting in isolation can also result in a failure to deliver a consistent message and coordinated intervention with families.

Developing effective multi-agency relationships involves understanding the different cultures, ethos, status, values and ideologies of agencies. In a safeguarding context, agencies are under the control of different government departments, which affects political and financial expectations. The professional history of each agency is also different, leading to subtle differences in perspective, expectation and practice. It is therefore important that time and sensitivity are given to communication between agencies in order to ensure clear understanding so that they can collectively take responsible for ensuring the safety and welfare of children.

Too much being expected of social workers

As discussed earlier, the pressures and demands on partner agencies can mean that they are not available to participate fully in safeguarding interventions, so it is not possible to achieve a multi-agency approach. This can mean that the majority of the intervention is undertaken by children's services social workers with other agencies having limited involvement, for example, taking responsibility for specific aspects of the child protection plan or contributing to conference. This has been acknowledged by Jan Horwath when she stated that 'social workers tend to take responsibility for assessment, decision-making and interventions, while other professionals take on "monitoring" and information-gathering roles'.[41]

It is common for social workers to meet on their own with families in order to gather information about their background, risks to the children and views of family members. The social worker will also produce an analysis of the situation and a plan to address risks which may be presented to a child protection conference, planning meeting or court. It is common for the chair of a meeting to look to the social worker to outline the situation and lead the discussion. Courts will also expect the social worker to file statements and plans in support of the local authority application and to give evidence at hearings. Other agencies often limit themselves to more factual reporting relating to their involvement but less commonly address the fundamental aspects of maltreatment to children, why this is occurring and action required. The role of the social worker may be further affected by limited multi-agency attendance at core groups and other meetings, meaning that information and opinions are not shared and coordinated to create a coherent picture of the family.

These elements often lead to social workers feeling very isolated and vulnerable. As discussed earlier, they may be required to balance many complex factors involving emotional challenges, dilemmas and conflicts. These include identifying risk factors, managing the responses and engagement of families, highlighting protective factors and ensuring that the plan for the safety and welfare of the children is effective. In this context social workers' thinking is expected to be clear, coherent, consistent, logical, proportionate and evidenced based. This creates enormous pressure and challenges for the social worker and it is easy to appreciate why, in isolation, they may not be able to adequately meet the demands being made of them. This can lead to a lack of focus on what maltreatment has occurred, how this can be addressed and progress which is being made.

There are many reasons why partner agencies may allow the social worker to take on the main burden of safeguarding practice. Children's services has the highest proportion of its services dedicated to safeguarding and it is legally and procedurally most accountable for the safety and welfare of children. Indeed the responsibility for taking legal action is almost entirely vested in children's services and they are likely to be held accountable for an inappropriate legal response regarding the safety and welfare of children.

Developing multi-agency approaches

In order for effective safeguarding practice to take place, it is necessary for social workers to have significant support and involvement from partner agencies. As already considered, this is a difficult area of professional development with all agencies experiencing reductions in resources and safeguarding practice having to compete with other priorities. It is therefore important that ways are found to involve partners which do not require them to commit significant additional resources.

To achieve this, the following four key areas are suggested for agencies to work supportively together and to improve significantly the focus and outcomes of assessing and planning. These four areas represent the development of respect, trust and understanding across agencies, which will serve to develop both healthy and effective relationships between agencies whilst modelling these elements to the family.

- *Gathering information:* It is important that agencies have the opportunity to contribute to all aspects of information gathering. For example, it is common for information to be requested from schools relating to a child's educational achievement, attendance and behaviour. However, this overlooks the potential insight and information which the school may have relating to much wider aspects of the family, including information and views regarding the child's emotional development, parenting capacity and environmental factors. Indeed, a classroom teacher who has taught a child for a term or so will probably be able to contribute significantly to all aspects of an assessment. By considering these, a relatively small amount of time can result in considerably improved information gathering.

- *Evaluation and analysis:* As already discussed, one of the key safeguarding requirements highlighted over recent decades is ensuring creative and reflective thinking relating to why a child is being harmed and how this can be addressed. Even with a highly skilled social worker, it is unlikely that they will be able to undertake this complex task on their own. It is much more likely to be achieved by a group of professionals, possibly in conjunction with family members, where ideas and opinions can interact and spark creative and reflective thinking. Individuals are often uncomfortable about coming to an evaluation and analysis of the situation and can feel vulnerable to being considered unfair or judgemental. In this context there is safety in numbers, where it is more likely that there can be challenge and exploration leading to a collective position to which all involved can feel confident and committed. It is also more likely that this process of evaluation and analysis will result in a balanced, proportionate, appropriate position which may be more persuasive in enabling professionals and the family to work together effectively to ensure the safety and welfare of children.

- *Core and planning groups:* As will be considered shortly, assessing and planning are processes in which information, commitment and interpretation of risks require continuous evaluation. It is important that consideration is given to changing circumstances relating to children and finding appropriate responses to this. Core groups are expected to be held at least every six weeks though they are often held more frequently. It is important that core groups and other planning meetings take collective responsibility for considering appropriate interventions and ensuring the safety and welfare of children. Reports to child protection conferences can be coordinated by the core group to reflect this joint responsibility. The nature of conflicting opinions, observations and information that remain unresolved should be presented to the conference with the reasons for each position. In this way the conference is able to examine a wider perspective, resolving the conflict in order to arrive at a planning position which may be accepted by professionals and the family.

- *Joint working*: As will be explored in Step Three, crucial to all safeguarding involvement is ensuring that change takes place with families which addresses the root problems and risk factors affecting the safety and welfare of children. Intervention with families to address these issues and motivate change is extremely challenging and less likely to be successful when attempted by a single practitioner or agency. Finding a helpful approach and having the courage to persevere and persist often requires intervention involving joint working. Whilst both practitioners can be from the same agency, there may be an added value if they have different professional backgrounds and can complement each other.

Developing relationships

As with all relationships, working effectively together will involve the development of rapport, respect, trust and understanding. Working in the manner outlined above will assist in this as professionals spend time together in face-to-face contact. Other forms of contact, for example by telephone and email, may be practical for straightforward communication but are probably less effective when addressing complex and delicate issues. There should be sufficient face-to-face communication with partner agencies to enable healthy and effective working relationships and a common sense of purpose.

It is inevitable that working closely in this manner will create conflict and disagreement. As discussed earlier, it is important that this is valued and understood as a natural aspect of a healthy and effective relationship and an opportunity to explore issues to find greater clarity and depth of involvement. Whilst every attempt should be made to resolve conflicts or disagreements, it may be necessary for the issue to be escalated to a manager, conference or court.

Developing effective multi-agency relationships also requires all safeguarding professionals to have an understanding of how other agencies operate. At the most basic level this will involve knowing about key individuals, structures and the agencies' priorities. It is important for professionals to be able to meet on a regular basis to develop professional understanding, practice and relationships. This may involve training events or liaison meetings where, in addition to the above, issues can be explored including:

- shared values, objectives and language
- when and how to make referrals
- ensuring early intervention
- eligibility criteria for assessment and services
- roles, functions and processes of each agency
- information sharing
- consistency in working practices
- developing joint approaches and co-working.

Early intervention

Children are most likely to benefit from safeguarding intervention if it takes place as early as possible in their life. This is a key message from the Munro Report. Graham Allen has highlighted that a child's brain is 25 per cent developed at birth and 80 per cent developed at the age of three years. He therefore concluded that any maltreatment or neglect to a child during this period is likely to have a profound and long-term effect on their development. Alternatively, intervention during this period which leads to consistent and appropriate parenting is likely to be particularly effective and important.[42]

Identifying young children who may be suffering maltreatment and neglect requires high levels of vigilance across all agencies and the public. An important aspect of this has been the Common Assessment Framework (CAF), which aims to identify children 'with additional needs' and work closely with carers to address these. The framework involves professionals who are closely involved with children to engage with their carers to complete a short assessment and identify a plan to address children's needs. This has led to a large number of children and carers being worked with by schools, children's centres and other services in order to prevent children becoming 'in need', as defined by section 17 of the Children Act 1989, or requiring the intervention of safeguarding services. Involvement under CAF requires the full agreement of carers and this appears to be very important in its effectiveness in offering support and services.

Working with adult services

An often neglected area of children's safeguarding work is the relationship with adult services, which work with a wide range of service users including those who are affected by mental health difficulties, learning disabilities, physical and sensory disabilities, substance misuse or due to being elderly. A considerable number of these service users are parents/carers and it is important that safeguarding and children's services are involved if the needs of the children are being affected by the carer's circumstances.

Working with adult services will involve consideration of how the needs of children and adults can best be met. Conflict can develop about the best way of doing this and, on occasions, adult and children's services can become polarised due to their primary focus being on the adult and child respectively. In these situations it is important to recognise that the children *and* adults are vulnerable individuals and services should be coordinated to ensure the most effective intervention. This may require shared funding and joint initiatives.

For example, a mother has a severe learning disability and has just given birth. Children's services are concerned about the mother's ability to offer suitable and consistent care to the baby and are seeking a mother and baby unit to monitor this closely. Adult services have been offering supported accommodation to the mother, but this is not considered appropriate for the baby. In this type of situation a unit could be considered which both meets the needs of the mother and the safety and welfare of the baby. In this situation it is crucial that social workers for the mother and the baby work closely together to find the right care arrangement so that funding is agreed which can enable this to be offered.

The welfare of children can also be a concern when they are considered to be a young carer for a vulnerable adult. Under the Carer (Recognition and Services) Act 1995, carers are entitled to a separate assessment to consider their ability to provide care, with a carer being defined as anyone who is offering 'regular and substantial' care. Children are often very committed to continuing to offer care. However, this can have a long-term effect on their physical, social, emotional and educational development. It is important therefore that the impact of caring is considered so that appropriate support and guidance can be offered. This is most likely to be effective if considered in conjunction with the assessment of the cared-for person and it is therefore important that adult and children's services jointly consider the family's circumstances and what support and assistance are required.

The relationship between children's and adult services is very well established in relation to children with disabilities who are considered to require services when they are over 18 years old. It is important that transition planning for these children is initiated as early as possible so that carers and children are aware of what will be available and are able to make choices about their options. Personalised budgets are very important for many children and adults with disabilities to enable them to have control over how funding is used to address preferences and the needs of the individual.

Summary of Step Two

Six things which children's services can do to develop a stable, skilled and confident workforce:

1. Undertake a confidential survey of the workforce to examine the level of morale and confidence. This should address issues such as workloads, emotional support, managerial guidance, professional development and how concerns are addressed. It is likely to be very helpful if the overall outcomes of this survey are discussed across the workforce so that barriers to achieving morale and confidence can be explored. This discussion should link to the issues, explored in Step One, relating to learning and change, motivation, developing relationships, styles of authority, responsibility and accountability.

2. Hold training sessions with all practitioners and managers to examine the 20 emotional challenges, dilemmas and conflicts of practice and how these can best be understood and acknowledged, giving consideration to how they may impact on best practice and the confidence of staff. These areas are inherent in safeguarding practice so, as they cannot normally be overcome or removed, the focus should be on being sensitive to them and developing personal and professional strategies to manage them.

3. Undertake a management review on how practitioners are professionally developed, monitored and supported. This should include considering the current and potential use of formal and informal supervision, coaching, practitioner observation, training,

practice guidance, case consultation, case audits, joint working and self-learning. Consideration should be given to how these can be combined to create an effective workforce strategy which addresses the skills and confidence of practitioners and ensures a high standard of practice.

4. Undertake an appraisal of all social workers, based on the 15 skill areas expanded from the Professional Capabilities Framework. This should identify areas of skill and areas of development in relation to each worker. These can then be amalgamated to provide a profile of the social worker workforce which can be used to identify training and development priorities for the agency as a whole. It is also important to consider workers' HCPC registration, date of last DBS disclosure, right to work in the UK and any issues relating to their physical or psychological ability to practise.

5. Introduce a procedure to address unacceptable behaviour and hold sessions with practitioners to focus on how they can work effectively with families whilst reducing the likelihood of an unacceptable behaviour incident. This should also involve ensuring that all incidents of unacceptable behaviour are managed to reduce the likelihood of further incidents, support the members of staff involved and maintain focus on the best interests of the child.

6. Hold meetings with partner agencies to explore effective ways of working together, including how agencies can be more involved in gathering information, evaluation, planning and working jointly. Consideration should also be given to developing a better understanding of the role, function and values of partner agencies, when and how to share information and when cases should be referred.

STEP THREE
Enable Families to Change

Enabling families to change to ensure the safety and welfare of children is the purpose and focus of all safeguarding intervention. This requires clarity about why a child is being mistreated or neglected and a strong sense of direction regarding what needs to change and how this can be achieved. Through this, contact with the family and partner agencies will have a clear focus, meaning that there is a coherent story about the family which is reflected in recording, assessing and planning. Progress should be constantly monitored to ensure that the best outcomes for children are achieved or, if this is not happening within reasonable timescales, consideration is given to identifying a more appropriate plan.

Continuous evaluation of risks and solutions

President Eisenhower stated 'I have never achieved anything without planning but have never seen a plan which achieved anything.'[43] In this he recognised on one hand the creative, reflective, active, flexible and continuous process of *planning*, whilst on the other hand the static, fixed and out-of-date aspects of a *plan*.

Safeguarding practice has arguably become too focused on assessments and plans which comply with a format and must be completed within a timeframe. It is important that safeguarding agencies are politically, publicly and professionally accountable and therefore a clear position on each case, in the form of an assessment and plan, is required. Having an assessment or plan is also an important reference point outlining the position at a given time and against which progress or changes can be evaluated. However, assessing and planning may only be full and accurate on the day of completion, and the circumstances of the family and risks to the children often change significantly, even within a few days. The assessment and plan can therefore offer a false sense of stability and may mean that full circumstances relating to the safety and welfare of the children may not be adequately recognised, leading to inappropriate responses.

The continuous evaluation of risks and solutions involves ensuring that, in addition to the formal assessment and plan, circumstances surrounding the risks to a child and how these can be addressed are subjected to constant assessing and planning. This will involve the following 13 areas. They should not be seen as sequential but rather as interacting, with each of these areas in a state of continuous change which impact on the other areas requiring these also to be re-evaluated. Understanding this state of flux is crucial to appreciating how risks to children and actions to address them are constantly changing. These 13 areas can also be used as a checklist when considering or reviewing cases as part of a child protection conference, visit to the family, core group, supervision, family group conference, case summary, transfer, referral, audit or legal planning meeting.

1. *There are constructive relationships with the family and partner agencies.*
    As discussed earlier, the quality of these relationships is crucial to ensure that all parties work effectively together to identify and resolve issues which are causing a child to be mistreated or neglected. Good relationships and rapport involve showing respect, value, trust and openness. It is important that there is effective communication with all key family members and partner agencies so that they feel consulted and part of the process of assessing and planning. This may involve the use of interpreters and translation of key information so that as much communication as possible is taking place in the family's preferred language.

2. *Key information is gathered from records, the family and partner agencies.*
    Sharing information requires trust and a belief that it will be used appropriately and constructively. Information should be shared between agencies in accordance with agreed protocols. The central aspect of information gathering is to determine maltreatment to the child, who appears most likely to have caused this, whether this is still occurring and the likelihood of it occurring in the future. It is important that historical information is considered as this may provide a useful insight into what may have contributed to the current situation and previous attempts to address issues. Chronologies should be used for showing key incidents and recurring patterns over time, ensuring that these are learnt from in the current situation. Consideration should be given to the family's faith, ethnicity, race and culture in order to

understand beliefs, values and perspectives which may be relevant to the concerns or finding solutions.

3. *The views of children, family members and partner agencies are gathered and considered.* This includes views about what has happened, why it has occurred and what action is required. As will be explored shortly, the views of the child are particularly important as these will assist in understanding the impact of the root problem and risk factors. It is often the views and interpretation of events which can create both creative thinking and conflict between family members and safeguarding professionals. Careful exploration should be made of views which are held and, as necessary, supported or challenged.

4. *Carer vulnerability is identified.* As already discussed, whilst safeguarding practice is fundamentally child centred, it is also important to highlight areas of vulnerability with family members who may require services in their own right. Examples would be mental health problems, substance dependency, physical disability, sensory impairment and learning disabilities/difficulties. Clearly these needs may impact directly on the child and therefore addressing them may result in the child being safeguarded. The needs of adults should be considered in relation to the needs of the child and it is important that planning is coordinated to ensure that the needs of each vulnerable individual are met without placing additional risk on other members of the family, particularly children.

5. *There is a clear understanding of resilience, strengths and protective factors.* All individuals have strengths and qualities which, if identified and utilised, can be significant in reducing the impact of root problems and risk factors. The resilience of children is also an important consideration. For example, the self-care skills of a 15-year-old may make them less vulnerable from neglect by their carer. It is also important that protective and supportive individuals are identified so that they can assist in addressing root problems and risk factors. The use of family group conferences and other network meetings can be very important in assessing and planning and in building support for change from family members.

6. *There is clear identification of root problems and risk factors relating to why a child is being harmed.* The root problems are those issues

which are fundamentally causing the child to be mistreated, for example carer misuse of alcohol or a violent relationship between carers. Identifying and addressing root problems and related risk factors is the most immediate and direct way to ensure the safety and welfare of the child. Root problems and risk factors may relate to very deep-seated issues, and addressing these may require considerable commitment on the part of the family and professionals. However, doing so is essential in ensuring change and the safety and welfare of the children. It is important to convince the carer of the need to change and to be clear about the likely action which will be considered if this is not achievable. It is also important to offer appropriate resources and support to enable change to take place.

7. *The impact, risk and experience of the child is understood and actively considered.* This area is central to ensuring that there is a focus on the best interests of the child. It is important to identify the specific risks to the child including the likelihood of these occurring and how the impact of these can be reduced. Consideration should be given to the current effect on the child and the likely impact over time. It is important to attempt to see the risks through the child's eyes, for example if the root problem relates to the carer's alcohol misuse, the impact on the child may include fear of losing their mother, being hungry, missing school and not having clean clothes/bedding. This child's perspective provides clarity and focus about the root problem and risk factors and can be very powerful in persuading the family of the level of risk, unacceptability of the current situation and need for change.

8. *Areas of uncertainty relating to information or understanding are identified.* These may relate to uncertainty on a wide range of issues including an individual's role, involvement in maltreatment of a child, level of personal skill, commitment and capacity to change. These uncertainties may also concern the complexity of the situation which requires further exploration or finding missing information. It is crucial that assumptions are not made about these areas of uncertainty. Areas of uncertainty often arise due to members of the family being reluctant to engage with professionals. Considerable skill and perseverance may be required to find an effective way to engage with these individuals.

9. *Areas of disagreement or conflict are resolved.* It is inevitable that there will be areas of disagreement or conflict and these should be

embraced as a natural part of exploration and understanding complex situations. It is important that the basis of disagreement and conflict are acknowledged and understood and that every effort is made to clarify or resolve these. It sometimes helps to consider the disagreement or conflict in light of the focus of ensuring the safety and welfare of the child. This can help identify areas of common agreement even if there may be different views about how this can best be achieved. Issues which cannot be resolved by the family and partner agencies should be referred to an appropriate manager or forum for consideration. In this way the area of disagreement or conflict is less likely to be divisive or adversely affect the relationship between professionals and families.

10. *There is analysis and evaluation of information and views.* This area considers all the information and views gathered and makes sense of them, highlighting key aspects. Consideration should be given to the evidence which supports information and views. It is crucial that a clear and coherent picture exists about the circumstances of the child and the risks which they present. This will involve creative and reflective thinking and the use of social work theory and research. Consideration should also be given to why the root problems and risk factors are occurring and how they can best be addressed. For example, if a mother's alcohol use is believed to relate to her own disrupted childhood, the plan to address the root problem of alcohol use may need to assist the mother come to term with aspects of her childhood.

11. *There is planning to address the root problems and risk factors.* This must focus on individuals' motivation and commitment to address the root problems and risk factors. It is important that the plan is clearly understood by all key family members and partner agencies. Ultimately, good planning is about 'putting your cards on the table', being clear about how the situation is being seen and identifying what needs to happen to address the root problems and risk factors. These issues may be difficult to address, but failure to focus on them will mean the child is likely to continue to be at risk. This is one of the fundamental challenges in safeguarding practice which must be grasped if planning is to be effective. It is crucial that there is clarity about evidence which will be gathered to identify whether the desired changes are taking place.

12. *Change is enabled to takes place.* Crucial to any change is being clear about what will be observable when the child is safe and well, including the behaviours and environmental factors which will be evident. Once the need for change has been identified it is crucial that there is a workable plan to bring about this change. For example, this may involve ensuring that a carer has access to resources such as substance misuse programme or mental health services. In many cases, however, the root problem will relate to lifestyle choices, for example the choice of relationships which affect the safety and welfare of the child. As will be explored shortly, a solution-focused approach is often found to be most effective with intervention focusing on an individual's strengths to build confidence and commitments to bringing about change.

13. *Progress is achieved in addressing root problems and risk factors.* The planning must be continuously monitored and evaluated to ensure that the child is acceptably safe and well during the period of intervention and that there is real change in relation to the root problems and risk factors. It is important that success is not measured by the tasks which have been completed but rather by the evidence that a child's safety and welfare have improved. It may not be necessary to totally eradicate the root problems and risk factors but sufficient progress should be identified which means that the child is receiving an acceptable level of care.

The problem and the solution

Throughout the 13 areas above consideration should be given to the balance between identifying the problem and finding solutions to address this. Safeguarding practice can sometimes focus too much on identifying the problem, involving extensive gathering and recording of information. This type of reporting and documentation is often about 'telling the story', for example giving accounts of maltreatment, incidents of concern and details of formal investigations. Such information gathering is important as it provides a record of the circumstances and evidence for the concern that can be used to evaluate change and ensure there is political, public and professionally accountable. Inspections and serious case reviews have often highlighted inadequate information gathering which has resulted in poor planning and missed opportunities to protect a child.

The difficulty with information gathering which focuses on the problem is that it is unlikely, on its own, to protect a child from further harm.

It amounts to taking stock of the situation but does not identify what is required to ensure the safety and welfare of the children and how this can be achieved. The 13 areas above aim to balance identifying the problem with finding solutions to address this.

It is important that there is a clear consensus between the family and safeguarding professionals regarding the nature of the problem, particularly regarding the root problems and risk factors, before a solution can be considered. There does not need to be total agreement but there must be reasonable common ground on which to consider what is required to change. Failure to achieve agreement on the nature of the problem will mean that there is unlikely to be sufficient commitment and motivation to change. There is a crucial point in assessing and planning when a shift is required from being focused on identifying the problems to finding solutions to address these. If this shift takes place too early there will be a lack of commitment, understanding and clarity of purpose. If the shift takes place too late or not at all there will be a lack of forward motion and solution. Therefore, if change is not taking place consideration should be given to whether there is sufficient consensus relating to why and how the child is being harmed and whether this insight is being used to identify solutions to addressing these.

Information gathering and coming to decisions

The overall process covered by the 13 areas above can also be considered as consisting of three main stages relating to how information is gathered and evaluated, leading to decisions relating to the safety and welfare of children. These three stages, which move practitioners from a broad and general view to a specific and focused one, are:

- *divergence* which involves gathering information from a wide range of sources and creating a broad picture of the situation

- *convergence* which involves discriminating between central and peripheral information so that there is focus and 'drilling down' with regards to important aspects

- *decision-making* which involves making choices about what has happened, the reasons for this and what is now required.

To take a simple example, if wishing to buy a television, it is likely that the *divergence* stage will involve information being gathered about possible models, including details of cost, quality and features. Following this, the *convergence* stage will involve choices being made relating to preferences, for example, setting a price limit and what quality is required. Finally, the *decision-making* will involve the television to be purchased, including decisions being made about options.

In a safeguarding context, the *divergence* stage involves information being gathered from records, partner agencies and the family. At this point it is uncertain what information is most relevant and therefore broad consideration is given to the situation from all angles. At this stage good listening skills and probing questions are very important. It is also particularly important to be open to all possibilities no matter how uncomfortable these may be. Once sufficient information has been gathered the *convergence* stage is when the most relevant information and circumstances are highlighted, enabling choices to be made about harm which has occurred, the most convincing explanations, root problems which have caused this and current risk factors. This may involve developing hypotheses or working theories regarding possible explanations. These are the focus for further information gathering and discussion in order to explore their validity. Following this, *decision-making* focuses on how root problems and risk factors can best be addressed. With new information, events, views and commitments, safeguarding practice requires the continuous process of divergence, convergence and decision-making.

It can be difficult for social workers to be confident as to when there is sufficient exploration and information available to move from divergence to convergence or from convergence to decision-making. Each of these requires some discrimination about what information is most important and possibly deciding that certain explanations or views are unconvincing or unlikely to be true. This can be uncomfortable and may lead to disagreement and conflict. Practitioners therefore require high levels of support and guidance to ensure that they are able to be clear when it is appropriate to move onto the next stage of the assessing and planning process.

Assessing risk

Risk assessment models are often based on considering the *likelihood* that an undesired event will take place and the *consequences* if this did occur. This model is based on the risk model used by insurance companies. For example, when offering a quote for motor insurance they will first consider aspects relating to the *likelihood* of a claim, including the age, experience and previous claims of the driver. Second, they will consider aspects relating to the financial *consequence* of a claim, including the value of the car and current costs of personal injury claims. By combining the likelihood and consequence factors a quote is calculated.

This model works well with situations where aspects relating to risk can easily be quantified. In a safeguarding context, it is useful in considering undesired events and identifying actions to reduce potential harm to a child. For example, if an undesired event is a child being left unsupervised and the root problem is her mother's use of alcohol, then the *likelihood* of this occurring can be reduced by the mother taking part in an alcohol programme which reduces her alcohol consumption. The *consequence* to the child if left unsupervised by her mother could be reduced if they live with a protective relative.

Managing uncertainty

Reducing risk by considering the likelihood and consequence of an undesired event may not be adequate in many safeguarding situations, if there is uncertainty about what may have happened and who caused harm to a child. In these situations consideration needs to be given to weighing up available information in order to come to a decision on the 'balance of probability'. This means that judgement is required based on what appears most likely to be true.

When a child receives a significant injury this matter is likely to be considered by a civil court which may decide that specialist assessments should take place, hear expert witnesses and spend days coming to a 'finding of fact' relating to what appears most likely to have happened. However, with most safeguarding cases, this level of scrutiny is not available and it is normally the responsibility of the social worker, in conjunction with other professionals, to weigh up evidence and come to a decision, on the balance of probability, about what action is required to ensure the safety and welfare of the child. For example, this may involve deciding that the child is 'suffering, or is likely to suffer, significant harm' (section 47, Children Act 1989) and a referral is made to a child protection conference, a meeting is held with the family under the Public Law Outline or, if the child is in immediate danger, an application is made to court.

Considering what is most likely, on the balance of probability, and deciding a course of action is particularly difficult when there is a high level of uncertainty or when evidence is inconclusive. There may be considerable anxiety about making a judgement, especially when there may be serious consequences. For example, a 12-month-old child has a broken arm and her mother is unable to provide an explanation about how this occurred, stating that her child regularly falls over. The medical examination concludes that the injury may have been caused non-accidentally. The child is placed with a foster carer whilst a child protection assessment is undertaken, and during this time the child is observed to be reasonably physically coordinated. The mother is considered to be loving and dedicated to her child but is often exhausted and has suffered from post-natal depression.

On one level it is easy to see why the social worker may choose to give the mother the benefit of the doubt and consider the injury as being caused by lack of supervision. There is no clear proof that the injury had been the result of physical abuse and it is humane and sympathetic to associate with the mother's stress and to wish to assist her during a difficult period. However, the medical evidence suggests non-accidental injury and it would appear that the child is not particularly accident prone. In this situation it could be argued that, on the balance of probability, the injury is likely to have been caused by the mother or another individual. However, even with this being likely, there is still a significant level of uncertainty and it is therefore difficult to conclude that the child should remain looked after by foster carers. Presuming that there are insufficient grounds to refer the matter to court and no further information is available to clarify the cause of the injury, then the child returning to the care of his mother may be a necessary, if uncomfortable, decision. Situations like these can be very divisive between professionals and families with often opposing views regarding the most appropriate action to take.

If it is decided that the child returns home, then it is likely that this would be under a child protection plan to monitor and support the mother. It is important that the level of uncertainty about the injury is clearly acknowledged so that there is high level of vigilance in terms of any further injuries to the child and the general level of care.

Ensuring fundamental change

Another key aspect of assessing risk is ensuring that fundamental change has taken place and therefore risks to the children have reduced to an acceptable level. As discussed earlier, change is often very difficult to achieve and many circumstances which place children at risk relate to very deep-seated lifestyle choices and emotional needs such as violent tendencies, dependence on substances and mental health problems. In a safeguarding environment which is focused on showing a reduction in risks to children, there can be a tendency to make assumptions which justify a view that change has taken place, even if this may not be supported by the evidence. This may be a temptation particularly if the consequences of the behaviour not changing lead to uncomfortable conclusions such as legal proceedings or the removal of the children from the family home.

For example, a father with two young children has repeatedly attacked his partner, causing bruising and cuts. Many of the incidents have been witnessed by the children who have also received minor injuries due to being hit by their father. The father left the family home during the child protection assessment and now wishes to return to his partner and children. He has started an anger management course and appears to have engaged well. The children are clearly missing their father and his return is seen as offering necessary support to his partner who is having difficulty coping in his absence. There have been no further incidents of violence and the father is considered to have managed the difficult situation calmly and appropriately. In this situation it can be tempting to see grounds which support a plan for the father to return home which would re-unify the family and alleviate the upset experienced by his partner and the children.

However, there are clear indications that the father may continue to present an ongoing danger to his family. Any inappropriate behaviour can be expected to reduce whilst safeguarding professionals are closely monitoring, meaning that the violent behaviour may return when the intensity of agencies' involvement reduces. The father's cooperation and attendance at the anger management course is to be welcomed. However, it should be considered whether this is likely to have identified the possibly deep-seated reasons for the behaviour and addressed them. It is also unclear whether the father will continue to be committed to work on finding ways to control his violent behaviour. Even so, there is a reasonable likelihood that the violent behaviour will continue, possibly on a reduced level.

This is a much more uncomfortable and challenging stance, which leads to a conclusion that it may not be safe for the father to live with his partner and children. There may not be any legal process for preventing the father's return to his partner unless she applies for a court injunction. If he were to return home then this is likely to be done under a child protection plan with close monitoring required. It is important that this fully acknowledges the potential risk to the children so that the work with the family is vigilant about new incidents which may further affect the safety and welfare of the children.

Managing anxiety and discomfort

These two examples illustrate some of the difficulties when assessing and planning become inconclusive or difficult to address. High levels of anxiety and discomfort can be experienced by professionals and families due to the combination of uncertainty and significant risks to children. This may lead to conflict and disagreement which, as discussed, need to be resolved. Alternatively, there may be a wish to avoid conflict and exploration of difficult issues. This can lead to agreements between professionals and families which are based on comfort and the avoidance of anxiety rather than the safety and welfare of the child.

In this situation strong leadership is required to enable professionals and family members to explore the complexity, conflicts and dilemmas of the case. This is likely to involve sharing and challenging views and interpretation of information in order to carefully weigh up the situation. This should lead to a collective view about the most likely root problems, risk factors and appropriate plan to address these. This exploration should be based on consideration of the 13, as outlined above, to ensure that all aspects of the case are taken into consideration.

Reviews of planning and progress

A considerable amount of activity and recording can be generated during involvement with families and it is important that this is reviewed on a regular basis to ensure that new information and changing circumstances are identified and the plan amended to ensure progress. Child protection conferences and other planning forums are a formal opportunity to review cases but more frequent interim reviews are necessary to ensure that the work is progressing appropriately and that the safety and welfare of the children are being addressed. Reviews can take place in supervision, core groups, coaching groups, visits to family and network meetings.

The 13 areas above are intended to assist in reviewing planning and progress but these can be summarised by considering whether there is clarity relating to:

- understanding the family and children's experiences, views and feelings
- the root problems and risk factors
- the plan to address the root problems and risk factors
- progress which is being made and how this ensures the safety and welfare of the children.

These reviews should be undertaken in conjunction with the responsible manager. If the child is not the subject of a child protection plan, consideration may be given to whether the child should be referred to conference or whether the case can be closed. If a child is the subject of a child protection plan then consideration can be given to convening a legal planning meeting and whether the child is safe to remain at home. Consideration should always be given to whether a copy of the review should be provided to the service user, child and partner agencies.

Ensuring the intervention is making a difference

It is common for social workers to presume that intervention will improve the safety and welfare of children. As discussed, the involvement of professionals is very likely to improve the quality and appropriateness of care being offered due to carers being more vigilant and responsive whilst being assessed and monitored. This change should not be presumed to be sustainable after safeguarding professionals are no longer involved with the family or when the intensity of involvement has reduced. Instead, consideration should be given to how carers are changing in terms of their purpose, identity and beliefs as this intrinsic change is a better indicator of positive new behaviour and lifestyle.

Consideration should also be given to whether the safeguarding intervention appears to be creating significant anxiety or aggravating the situation. This may happen in the short term, for example due to the shock of the initial intervention or painful issues being raised by the involvement of services. The process of change can also involve periods when the situation is perceived to be getting worse. These issues may need to be worked through before the benefits can be realised and it is important that safeguarding professionals monitor the safety and welfare of children closely during these periods.

A further possibility is that the intervention is having little or no impact on the safety and welfare of the children. At first this may appear a depressing conclusion, especially if considerable effort has been expended. The chances of intervention having an impact can be increased significantly if based on a clear analysis of the problem. However, even with careful planning, some interventions will still not be effective. One of the most important aspects of safeguarding is the ability to recognise that the intervention is not being effective or appears unlikely to be effective.

Albert Einstein stated that 'insanity is doing the same thing over and over again and expecting different results'[44] It may be more helpful not to think of the intervention as a failure but rather providing evidence of what has not worked so that alternative, successful interventions can be identified. For example, a plan may focus on a mother attending sessions to address her use of alcohol. However, when reviewed, it is discovered that she has not attended these sessions. At one level this could be seen as an action which has not been met. Whilst it may be appropriate to give the mother a second chance to prove her commitment to attend the sessions, it is important not simply to rerun the same action, which may mean the likelihood of a similar outcome. Instead it may be necessary to *do something different.*

In this example, it may be as simple as clarifying the reasons for the mother not attending the sessions so that additional support can be considered. It may also be necessary to increase the mother's motivation by restating the reasons for the sessions and what may happen if she continues not to engage with the service. The important thing is to learn from the action which is not being successful and to ensure that creative thinking can come out of this apparent failure. As with all change, success may not happen on the first attempt and some perseverance and creative learning may be required in order to make progress.

Ensuring root problems and risk factors are addressed

It is important that all interventions are based on addressing the root problems which have led to risk factors and that success is measured by how risk factors have reduced due to the root problems being addressed.

For example, a six-year-old child is being neglected by his mother. The child receives very little stimulation and is undernourished. He has become difficult to manage at school, losing his temper and attacking other children. The assessment concludes with a hypothesis that the neglect is related to the mother's mental health problems. She has not attended appointments with mental health professionals or taken medication. A plan is agreed which includes:

- the social worker making a referral to Children and Adolescent Mental Health Services (CAMHS)

- the social worker visiting the family every two weeks

- the mother being referred to parenting classes.

All of these actions relate directly to the presenting difficulties, which are the neglect of the child and his behaviour issues. They are likely to be beneficial to the child and therefore may be presumed to improve the safety and welfare of the child. However, there may be little prospect of long-term change unless the root problem, relating to the mother's mental health difficulties, is addressed.

The focus must therefore relate to the mother receiving an assessment and taking her prescribed medication. If the hypothesis is valid, then addressing these issues should mean that there is evidence that the child is receiving more appropriate care from his mother and indications that the child's behaviour is improving at school.

It is also possible that even with the mother's mental health stabilised, the child continues to be neglected and show behavioural difficulties. This suggests that the hypothesis may not be valid and that the neglect relates to aspects other than the mental health problems. For example, the mother may have deep-seated emotional difficulties which may have led to both the neglect of the child *and* the mental health difficulties. So the mental health difficulties are not directly causing the neglect of the child and therefore this cannot be addressed through a focus on the mental health difficulties. The importance of realising this is that a new hypothesis can be suggested that the neglect of the child relates to the more fundamental emotional issues which will need to be addressed. Doing so is likely to address both the mental health difficulties and the neglect of the child. This is an example of where clear evaluation and reflection can lead to recognition that expected outcomes have not been achieved and an understanding of the reasons for this. This insight can be used to agree a new hypothesis and planning to find an effective solution to the presenting difficulties.

Cases which are not progressing

Due to the complexity of safeguarding practice and the emotional challenges, dilemmas and conflicts inherent in it, it is easy to see how cases may not adequately progress in effectively identifying and addressing root problems and risk factors. In order to address these 'stuck' cases, support and challenge need to be available to social workers so that creative and reflective thinking can be developed to find workable solutions to progress the case.

As discussed, it is essential that no one practitioner, for example, the social worker, feels that they are on their own to find a solution as it is less likely that they will be able to resolve the complexity of the issues. The general principle should be that the more 'stuck' a case is then the more practitioners, managers and family members should be available to help find ways to explore what is inhibiting progress and how these can be overcome. There can be 'safety in numbers', which means that a group can take joint responsibility for exploring the complexity of the issues and identifying actions, even if this solution is challenging or likely to be unpopular to some. The involvement of a responsible manager is essential in ensuring that the necessary decisions are made. These discussions can take place in:

- coaching sessions with a group of social workers
- extended supervision, involving a number of professionals
- groups of professionals who may have specialist insight or knowledge
- core groups
- case review forums which meet regularly to explore cases
- child protection conferences and other network meetings.

Whilst resource intensive, this approach is likely to prevent inappropriate or ineffective intervention and save time and resources in the longer term. It can also lead to important decisions being made relating to services, the nature of interventions and legal action.

Effective approaches with families

It is important to remember that individuals cannot be made to change. Enabling relationships involves creating opportunities to see patterns of unhelpful behaviour and belief, and exploring choices which can be made. This requires the enabler to be patient, resilient, responsive and persistent. At the heart of all good assessing and planning is the ability to feed back observations and ask powerful questions which delve deeper into the issues and enable professionals and families to reflect on past and current situations in order to find a focus for change.

All of the issues addressed in Step One are relevant to developing effective approaches with families. The following approaches focus these issues further, specifically in the context of enabling families to change.

Fear and anxiety of families

Working in a direct and honest way with families is probably one of the most challenging aspects of safeguarding practice. It is emotionally charged and, no matter how sensitively issues are broached, the intervention by social workers may lead carers to be anxious and uncertain. This may relate to being seen as poor carers or feelings of embarrassment, guilt and shame. Carers may also be anxious about decisions which may be made about their children, in particular the chance that they will be removed. Whilst legal proceedings are very rare, some carers may even fear, based on media stories, that their child may be removed from their care without notice or adequate recourse.

Even if anxiety and uncertainty are low and manageable, they may still make it more difficult for the carer to be open and trusting with social workers and other safeguarding professionals. Distress experienced by families may require support and time to enable them to accept the concerns which are being raised about their children and to fully engage with professionals. Anxiety and uncertainty can cause individuals to respond in a number of ways, meaning that initial contact can be very difficult. They may freeze, meaning that they are unable to respond to what is being said, and this may be interpreted as not taking concerns seriously or failing to engage. Alternatively, they may become defensive or deny what is being suggested and this may be interpreted as being unreasonable or not accepting responsibility. These responses may also involve a range of emotions including being attacking, upset, accusatory, evasive or hostile.

So these responses, triggered by shock or the need to absorb and comprehend the situation, may not be a good indicator of how an individual normally behaves. However, they can start a relationship 'on the wrong foot' and sensitive management of this may be necessary to establish a constructive working relationship in the longer term. In order to ensure a healthy and effective relationship with carers, appropriate levels of reassurance may need to be provided. Initially it may help if social workers simply acknowledge that the family may be anxious about the involvement. An explanation can be given about broadly what is required to happen so that the carer can be more receptive to the issues which require attention. It may also help if social workers explain their intention to work in partnership to establish a relationship based on fairness and balance. Once the initial anxiety has reduced, most families will want information about the concerns and will appreciate an honest and direct approach which also aims to be sensitive, appropriately reassuring and open to understanding the family's views and circumstances.

This is similar to visiting a doctor to discuss a potentially serious concern. Whilst highly anxious, most people will want clear information about the situation and options which are available. If an unpleasant procedure is being proposed, the patient may particularly need to know about alternatives and the relative merits of these. The focus is likely to be on the long-term benefits rather than the short-term unpleasantness. Honesty, sensitivity and reassurance are important in these situations and there is a need to consider how the process can be made most comfortable.

Empathy and sympathy

Both empathy and sympathy involve high levels of respect, affection, compassion and understanding and can therefore easily become confused. It is important to consider the dynamics which relate to each as this is important in developing an appropriate relationship between professionals and families.

Empathy involves understanding and appreciating another person's feelings and opinions and how these relate to their behaviour. It involves expecting the individual to account for what they have done or failed to do and supporting them to recognise and respond to the situation in which they now find themselves. This keeps the individual at the heart of decision-making, supported to explore ways to move forward. This is consistent with coaching, action learning and leadership approaches which focus on assisting individuals find their own solutions.

Sympathy relates to a closer emotional relationship, which involves jointly associating with and sharing feelings. This often involves one individual taking on the mood, views and feelings of another. This is therefore less likely to involve challenge or assisting an individual to consider accountability, responsibility or to re-think their position. Whereas empathy can be seen as 'helping an individual get out of a hole', sympathy can be seen as 'getting into the hole with the individual'. In a safeguarding context, sympathy is of limited value as it blurs personal boundaries and therefore is unlikely to enable positive change.

Clarity about intervention

Developing an effective relationship with families involves being clear about the purpose and focus of the involvement. This will include having honest and open discussion with families and providing them with copies of assessments and care plans, ensuring that these are translated or read in families' preferred language. Children can also receive a copy of the assessment and plan, following consideration of their age and understanding. Sections may need to be removed if they relate to a third person or if sharing the material is not considered to be in the child's best interests.

In addition, it can be very helpful to provide carers with a formal letter outlining what is expected of them and the focus of the intervention. This letter should acknowledge that the current situation may be difficult or uncomfortable for the family and convey the intention to work constructively to understand the family and address concerns in order to ensure the safety and welfare of their children. It is important to emphasise that the relationship is a collaborative one and that the views, feelings and experiences of the family will be welcomed and respected. The letter should include details of the nature of the working relationship, expectations of the family and what they can expect from professionals. Appendix D contains further details of what the letter might contain, including issues which are relevant when a child is the subject of a child protection plan.

This letter should be given to the carers so that its content can be verbally reinforced. Carers may be asked to sign a slip to confirm that they have received and understand the contents of the letter. Reference may later be made to the letter if concerns continue, for example, if an application is made to court. A copy of the letter may also be given to children, following consideration of their age and understanding. Whether or not a copy is given, it is very useful to discuss or provide children with a summary of key points and actions.

Purposeful visits and meetings

Considerable time and resources are spent on visits and meetings. For these to contribute to a successful outcome it is essential that they have a clear purpose and focus and ensure that all children, especially those who are the subject of a child protection plan, are safe and well. At the start of all visits and meetings it is often helpful for the main focus and purpose of the intervention to be restated with an update of key developments. Any changes in circumstances should be carefully considered so that changes can be made to services and interventions. It is crucial that social workers and other safeguarding professionals are particularly vigilant to any bruising, marks or injuries to a child or adult in the household.

All visits and meetings should be planned and structured in relation to the root problems in order to reduce risks factors. This will mean that social workers will probably attend each visit or meeting with several objectives to be achieved. For example, if the case involves a mother who was neglecting her children due to a dependency on alcohol, a visit may focus on:

- making observations about the cleanliness of the home, if this is a tangible indication of the level of alcohol use

- discussing attempts to limit or reduce alcohol use

- meeting with the children to assess the level of care being offered and whether they are feeling settled and secure.

In all visits and meetings it is important to consider how family members communicate and behave towards professionals. This includes whether they are being consistent, honest and sharing key information or whether they appear to be evasive or avoiding issues. It should always be remembered that appearing to be open, cooperative and compliant does not necessarily mean that children's safety and welfare is being addressed. Along with considering how family members are relating, there must be vigilance about evidence which confirms the level of care being offered to the child. As will be explored shortly, it is essential that this involves working directly with children.

At the end of the visit or meeting it is also often helpful to summarise what has been discussed and the actions agreed. This is often a good time to offer feedback to members of the family. Some family members may find it helpful to know what will be recorded and what information will be shared or discussed with other agencies.

It is common for practitioners to make a visit or attend a meeting and to find the family in a state of crisis about an immediate issue which they are facing. For example, a disconnection of electricity notice may have been recently received and is causing anxiety. Not to address this immediate issue may be counter-productive as it could give the impression of not being empathetic. However, having the plan for the visit being side-stepped is also not helpful as it would mean the key purpose of involvement is not being followed. In this situation it would be reasonable to split the time available for the visit or meeting so that the crisis issue and the planned reasons for the visit are both addressed.

Use of questionnaires and scales

Engaging with families can be challenging and it is useful to gather information and understanding through the use of a range of techniques which help build trust and rapport. There are many tools available from publications and websites, for example the Department of Health recommends the use of the following questionnaires and scales to enable work with families.

- *The Strengths and Difficulties Questionnaires* on emotional and behavioural issues

- *The Parenting Daily Hassles Scale* on the frequency and intensity of anxieties and challenges experienced by carers

- *Home Conditions Scale* on the physical condition of the home

- *Adult Wellbeing Scale* on carers in terms of their anxiety, depression and irritability

- *The Adolescent Wellbeing Scale* on the feelings of adolescents.

It is important that questionnaires and scales are not seen as tools to be completed but rather as an opportunity to explore issues with family members. The most useful part of using these may not be what is recorded but rather the interaction and process of exploring these issues. It should always be remembered that these are tools to enable the 13 areas of continuous evaluation.

Use of solution-focused brief therapy

Over recent years, solution-focused brief therapy (SFBT) has become popular in safeguarding practice across many countries. The approach was developed in California during the 1960s and has been established in the UK since the late 1980s. It is the theoretical foundation of the Signs of Safety model, which is used in many child protection conferences.

SFBT addresses the purpose and focus of the intervention by inviting individuals and families to identify their 'best hopes', looking forward to what they want to achieve. In many therapeutic relationships this would be defined by the recipient of the service. However, in a safeguarding context it is essential for this to be negotiated between social workers and the family. What is important is that all those involved with the intervention agree the focus and how this ensures the safety and welfare of children. By developing this clarity of purpose, families and professionals are more likely to find the commitment and motivation to make changes which address the concerns.

The approach is based on the assumption that individuals are resourceful and, with guidance, encouragement and support, can find their own solutions. The focus is therefore on what can realistically change rather than on intractable elements. Whilst it is crucial that there is a clear understanding of the problem, real change is only going to happen if the focus is balanced with finding solutions to the problems. Families often find it easier to discuss solutions as these relate to thinking forward to a time when concerns and anxieties have reduced. This involves focusing on levels of cooperation and motivation to improve the situation, including progress which has already been made and resources which are available.

SFBT has been evidenced to be very effective in a safeguarding context. Some of the reasons for this may be that the approach is very empowering for families and invites them to take responsibility and control of a more positive future, enabling them to collaborate and find tangible strategies for achieving this. It aims to find strengths and abilities, with even very small progress and success being used to build confidence and hope about the likelihood of further change.[45]

Working with children

To facilitate working with children, social workers should have a sound knowledge of child development, engagement skills and a range of tools to enable communication. These are readily available and can help practitioners to 'break the ice' and find a reasonably comfortable working environment. These skills and knowledge need to relate to engaging with all children from toddlers to adolescents. Consideration should always be given to the speed with which the child is able to develop trust and become open about their views, feelings and experiences.

This will require patience and sensitivity and it is important that time is allowed for professionals to engage with children. With the introduction of the single assessment, practitioners now have up to 45 working days to complete an assessment. This allows a reasonable period of time to enable a number of sessions with children so that trust and confidence can be developed.

It is presumed that the social worker will be responsible for ensuring that the views, feelings and experiences of children are considered. However, it is very important that other safeguarding professionals are also involved and consideration is given to who is in the best position to undertake certain elements of the work.

In addition, when working with a group of children in a family it is important to develop this work with each child. It is common for one or more children to feature less in the involvement with the family, particularly with large sibling groups spanning a considerable age range and need. Working with children is a significant demand on the time and energy of practitioners, and they and their managers must consider how this work can be undertaken.

Initially, engaging with children is often easier if the focus is on the child's views, feelings and experiences as these relate to general issues rather than to aspects connected to maltreatment or neglect. For example, it can be helpful for the practitioner to consider issues such as the child's:

- favourite food
- friends and key people
- family members and relatives
- experiences at school or nursery
- daily routines
- sleeping arrangements and clothes storage
- favourite toys, games, hobbies and interests
- best days out and holidays
- arrangements for completing homework
- pets.

These tangible elements can help to construct a picture of what life is like for the child on a day-to-day basis. This will assist in identifying areas of need and risk, but as most of these issues are less likely to be sensitive, they also offer an opportunity initially to spend time directly with the child in order to develop trust and rapport.

However, for safeguarding work to really incorporate the best interests of the children, the impact of maltreatment or neglect must also be understood from the child's perspective. Such experiences can leave the child confused, insecure, frightened, anxious and uncertain so careful consideration should be given to the timing and most appropriate approach to addressing these sensitive issues. There are many techniques and approaches which have been developed to assist in communicating with children with consideration given to the child's age, understanding and emotional strengths. These are easily found in publications and on websites.

Incorporating the views, feelings and experiences into planning

Information learnt from direct work with children must be considered as part of assessments, core groups, supervision, case summaries, chronologies, conferences, planning meetings and legal proceedings. It is only in this way that the views, feelings and experiences of the child can be fully incorporated into assessing and planning.

The involvement of children in conferences, reviews and planning meetings is important in ensuring that their voice is central to the work. For older children this will involve considering the style and organisation of these meetings so that they can fully participate. Some meetings or parts of meetings are not appropriate for children to attend, for example, if a carer's childhood experiences are to be discussed and it is not felt to be in the child's interests to be aware of this. If a child is not to be present at a meeting then their views, feelings and experiences can be identified and presented to the meeting on behalf of the child by a trusted family member or professional.

Access to advocacy services and Independent Visitors is important for some children and consideration should be continuously given to how these can be used to enable the child's voice to be heard. The views, feelings and experiences of children should also be a standard item on the agenda of all meetings relating to children. Following these meetings it is also important for the child to receive age-sensitive feedback about what was discussed and how professionals are intending to safeguard the child's safety and welfare. The process for feeding back to children should be considered by the meeting, including the timing and who is best placed to do it.

Defining progress

A final and important aspect of ensuring that the best interests of children are met relates to whether real progress has been made in the safeguarding intervention. As discussed earlier, performance management systems often aim to measure progress and successful interventions through the frequency and timeliness of aspects such as assessment, visits to the family and supervision. However, a more substantial and valuable measure of success is how children are reporting change to their views, feelings and experiences. Children's sense of stability and security are arguably the most important indicators of successful safeguarding interventions and any monitoring of effectiveness and success must therefore include how children are reporting their perception of the impact of the intervention.

Summary of Step Three

Five things which children's services can do to enable families to change:

1. Hold sessions with practitioners and managers to explore how the 13 areas of continuous evaluation of risk and solutions can best be used to ensure effective assessing and planning. This should consider developing clarity about the root problems and risk factors, how these can be addressed and how to ensure progress is being made in addressing them. This will involve considering information gathering, working effectively with families and finding the balance between identifying the 'problem' and finding 'solutions'.

2. Following these sessions, audit a sample of cases to consider whether there is evidence of the issues above influencing effective safeguarding interventions. Consideration should also be given to the purposefulness of visits and meetings, evaluating whether these have enabled families to learn and change.

3. Identify a number of cases where there is significant uncertainty about risks to a child, disagreement between professionals or challenges to achieving change. Consideration should be given to holding case consultation meetings to examine what approaches have been deployed, the basis of uncertainty, how anxiety is being managed, achieving consensus and identifying how the case can be successfully progressed.

4. Implement a procedure and guidance which ensures that a standard letter is sent to all carers outlining the nature and expectations of the intervention. Audits of cases should consider whether these letters have been successful in establishing clarity about the intervention and facilitating families to engage with professionals to ensure the safety and welfare of their children.

5. Audit a sample of cases to examine direct involvement with children to consider how often the child was seen, the flexibility of the approach, the pace of sessions and what techniques were used to facilitate them. Consideration should also be given to how the information from these sessions influenced the planning on the case and was used as part of the qualitative performance management framework.

APPENDIX A

Checklist for social worker appraisal based on the Professional Capabilities Framework (PCF)

The following checklist can be used for appraising a practitioner's skills, and identifying their areas of strength and development. The capabilities are those developed by the College of Social Work and the Social Work Reform Board and is now owned by the College of Social Work.

Capability 1: Professionalism – Identify and behave as a professional social worker, committed to professional development

To what extent does the social worker:

- place the welfare of children at the centre of their practice
- understand the difference between personal and professional boundaries
- behave appropriately and in a manner fitting to the situation
- understand their authority and use information to make decisions or recommendations
- show accountability and take responsibility for their views, decisions and actions
- present information in a clear, thorough, transparent, proportionate, consistent and logical manner
- respond to telephone calls, letters, emails and other communications in an appropriate and timely manner
- show commitment to continuing professional development, reflect on their practice and set learning goals

- use scheduled supervision appropriately to discuss issues, progress and request guidance/decisions
- know when to seek urgent consultation with a manager to discuss new significant information, difficulties with meeting timescales and request guidance/decisions
- understand how emotional challenges, anxiety and conflicts can distort clear thinking
- ensure they keep themselves personally as safe as possible whilst still being effective in their intervention
- recognise and challenge poor practice and unacceptable conduct
- manage conflicting priorities and, when necessary, balance competing tasks
- keep track of several different tasks at the same time?

Capability 2: Values and ethics – Apply social work ethical principles and values to guide professional practice

To what extent does the social worker:

- recognise the unacceptable nature of the maltreatment of children
- treat all individuals with respect, dignity and value and show sensitivity to the views and backgrounds of others
- promote positive relationships with partner agencies and families
- follow principles of confidentiality
- appreciate how their values and beliefs may be similar to or different from others' and ensure that this is not used to judge others as being right or wrong
- undertake the best possible job and follow principles of best practice, given available resources and skills
- believe that individuals have the potential, with direction and support, to improve their situation and change behaviour, outlook and priorities
- understand and promote the legal, moral and procedural rights of individuals
- understand and develop their values and principles

- work within legal and statutory requirements
- resolve challenges, conflicts and dilemmas
- respond in an appropriate manner to complaints and enquiries from service users, professionals, advocates, members of parliament, councillors and the ombudsman?

Capability 3: Diversity – Recognise diversity and apply anti-discriminatory and anti-oppressive principles in practice

To what extent does the social worker:

- understand how individuals can suffer discrimination and oppression due to their race, religion, culture, lifestyle choices and other aspects of their personal background
- understand their authority's equality and diversity strategy
- consider, understand and respect an individual or family's background, abilities, sexual orientation, gender, ethnicity, faith, culture, race, value base, age and beliefs, including how these factors are relevant to current circumstances and planning
- respect and value difference
- challenge their own attitudes and perceptions
- show understanding of how their own background may create dynamics with those of a different background
- value and actively encourage the contributions and opinions of all groups and individuals
- challenge discrimination, oppression and cultural assumptions
- work in partnership with interpreters to ensure a clear understanding and communication with families when English is not their first language
- ensure all materials are translated or interpreted so that they can be understood in an individual's preferred language and advise on alternative options/facilities to ensure equality of access to information and services
- seek feedback and actively encourage the involvement of different groups in the development of services?

Capability 4: Rights, justice and economic well-being – Advance human rights and promote social justice and economic well-being

To what extent does the social worker:

- understand the impact of poverty
- enable individuals to be heard and take their views/perspectives into consideration
- understand how poverty and lack of opportunity can impact on the ability to care for and protect children
- enable individuals and families to access resources and services
- enable economic well-being and independence through access to benefits, education and employment
- use advocates and specialist advisors to promote the opportunities and involvement of individuals
- challenge practice and policy which is directly or indirectly disadvantaging individuals
- understand the role of legal challenge, including the use of judicial reviews?

Capability 5: Knowledge – Apply knowledge of social sciences, law and social work practice theory

To what extent does the social worker:

- understand and use legislation, regulations, guidance, procedures and protocols
- apply theory and research appropriately to improve need/risk identification and planning
- understand the process and content of assessments, reports for court, conference and other meetings
- meet timescales
- understand the principles behind practice so that there is a framework to resolve and understand difficult issues
- understand the stages of child development from 0 to 18 years
- understand the structure, role and function of children's services, other local authority departments and partner agencies

- have a good knowledge of local and national resources
- understand and use eligibility criteria and thresholds for services and how to make referrals?

Capability 6: Critical reflection and analysis – Apply critical reflection and analysis to inform and provide a rationale for professional decision-making

To what extent does the social worker:

- continuously evaluate, analyse, probe and consider information in order to come to an evidenced and balanced view about why a child has been mistreated, and undertake planning to address this
- use research and theory to inform practice and planning
- listen with a 'constructive ear' to identify the true nature of what is being said or withheld and the relevance of statements and behaviour
- understand various forms of risk and vulnerability and be vigilant about indicators of harm
- highlight the most important aspects of a case and ensure that these do not get lost in the detail
- evaluate the likelihood of various explanations and the reliability of information in order to make a proportionate and balanced response to these
- weigh up the likelihood and consequences of undesired events, taking into consideration protective and risk factors
- provide a clear rationale for judgements and decisions
- appreciate the urgency of information and situations and what immediate action may be required
- differentiate between information and opinion
- place information, views and risks within the wider context of the family's background, race, culture, lifestyle, values and beliefs
- appreciate the potential risks associated with various interventions and be able to reduce these as far as is feasible
- present verbally and in writing their critical, reflective and analytical thinking, supporting this with evidence and observations?

Capability 7: Intervention and skills – Use judgement and authority to intervene with individuals, families and communities to promote independence, provide support and prevent harm, neglect and abuse

A. Developing healthy and effective relationships.

To what extent does the social worker:

- develop rapport and communication with families, including being able to value, respect, listen, understand and empathise

- ensure they are understood by others and able to present information effectively, structuring and sequencing this appropriately

- write accurately, logically, clearly and concisely

- contribute effectively to meetings

- listen and be open and responsive when receiving information

- ensure there is a clear purpose in all cases based on addressing root problems and risk factors

- display tact, sensitivity and diplomacy in all situations and be able to vary style, language and method according to the audience

- communicate with children, taking into consideration their stage of development, age and understanding

- focus on strengths, commitments, views and insights

- understand the effects of mental health problems, drugs/alcohol/ substance misuse, domestic violence, emotional/learning difficulties and physical/sensory disabilities as they relate to carers, children or other individuals

- use agreements with the family to clarify the nature of the involvement and expectations

- know when and how to explore key issues in a sensitive and effective way

- maintain an approach which considers the validity, accuracy and honesty of what they are being told

- persevere and find effective and creative ways to engage with individuals who may be anxious, angry, fearful, erratic, evasive, overwhelmed, defensive and hard to engage

- work with those who are violent, aggressive, hostile and threatening, including knowing when to engage with individuals and when to recognise that there is an unacceptable level of personal danger and protective action is required

- ensure they are clear and consistent about what is expected from families and partner agencies whilst also being open to changing situations, views and perspectives

- explore difficult issues and lead discussion with families and partner agencies in order to deepen understanding

- promote confidence and independence

- persuade individuals of the need to change, enabling them to understand and be committed to planning?

B. Assessment.

To what extent does the social worker:

- ensure appropriate amounts of information are gathered from case files, partner agencies and the family

- gather information in a manner which summarises and focuses on key areas

- minimise duplication of information

- engage with children in an appropriate manner to ensure that their experiences, views and feelings are taken into consideration

- use chronologies to ensure there is clarity about events over time

- use assessment tools, for example genograms, eco-maps, questionnaires and scales

- consider the social, religious and ethnic background of the family

- identify missing or unclear information

- identify areas of resilience, strength and protective factors

- consult with and inform the family and partner agencies of the likely conclusion of assessments so that they are able to respond to these before the assessment is completed

- make logical, evidenced and clear conclusions based on available information and opinions

- think flexibly, reflectively and creatively in order to make professional judgments, in conjunction with the family and partner agencies
- clearly identify root problems and risk factors
- hypothesise, evaluate and analyse information to draw out the most important aspects of the case and weigh up the likelihood and consequences of potentially harmful events
- ensure there is a clear care plan which addresses the root problems and risk factors and that this plan is followed?

C. Ensuring planning for children.
To what extent does the social worker:

- offer support and guidance to enable necessary changes to take place
- understand what will enable and prevent change taking place
- negotiate and take into consideration conflicting views/positions and be able to find ways to respect, value and resolve these
- review the effectiveness of plans
- prepare for sessions and have a clear plan for what is required from visits, meetings, etc.
- use supervision and management consultation to address issues where the plan is not progressing
- make referrals to other agencies
- use pre-meeting discussion, for example over the telephone, to negotiate and prepare for a constructive visit or meeting
- manage situations where others have alternative priorities or conflicting views
- recommend alternative action if the plan is not progressing in a timely manner, including the use of legal planning meetings
- consider whether cases can be 'stepped down' to children in need plans or CAFs?

D. Ensuring progress on the plan.
To what extent does the social worker:

- ensure that all visits and meetings consider new information and how root problems/factors are being addressed

- view assessing and planning as a continuous process where information, risks, opinion, insight and commitment are constantly evolving and changing
- work closely with partner agencies to share information and views in order to develop planning
- use core groups, network meetings and conferences to engage fully with partner agencies and ensure that issues are discussed and responsibility shared
- identify the indicators which ensure that a child's safety and welfare are improving
- recognise that fundamental change is more likely to happen if the family is focused on future outcomes
- enable the family to define their 'best hopes' for the future, which includes ensuring the safety and welfare of their children
- focus on progress which has been made and what the family members have done to achieve this in order to increase confidence and responsibility
- understand that lack of commitment and motivation from the family and partner agencies may relate to the intervention approach which is being used and that this may need to be reconsidered
- ensure that important information is recorded immediately and shared with key individuals and managers
- show clarity about the legal processes which may be required if an acceptable level of change cannot be achieved within reasonable timescales?

Capability 8: Context and organisation – Engage with, inform and adapt to changing contexts and shape practice. Operate effectively within own organisation's framework and within multi-agency settings to contribute to the development of services and organisations

A. Maintaining a customer focus.

To what extent does the social worker:

- consistently demonstrate a clear understanding of customers' needs and requirements

- accurately record customer needs/views and act promptly to resolve requests or problems

- understand service standards, customer care standards and complaints procedures

- demonstrate the ability to listen, convey interest and understand

- show empathy and sensitivity when dealing with customer requests and resolve these effectively

- seek customer feedback and change practice in response to this

- develop an in-depth understanding of customer requirements and identify opportunities to add value and deliver a more effective, quality service?

B. Working within children's services and with partner agencies.
To what extent does the social worker:

- work readily with others to achieve aims and objectives, ensuring that these are clear to others

- develop a climate of trust and openness

- show consideration for others' needs and feelings

- value achievement, good ideas and the contribution of others

- share information, ideas and feelings with colleagues

- build respectful and trusting relationships within their team and with partner agencies

- resolve conflicts and differences of opinion with partner agencies and, if necessary, refer the matter to more senior management for consideration

- ensure that relevant individuals and services are involved and understand their role

- encourage team developments in order to improve performance

- respond positively to requests for help and support

- contribute to organisational policy and practice

- understand the role of partner agencies and their perspective, priorities, regulations, systems, resources, pressures and processes

- share information across agencies in accordance with local and national protocols and guidance

- keep partner agencies informed of developments in cases and ensure their involvement?

C. Recording and reporting.

To what extent does the social worker:

- make appropriately detailed records, reports, assessments, letters and emails

- write in a style which is clear and easy to understand, avoiding ambiguity or potential for misinterpretation

- ensure that reports and records are written and structured in a style which is appropriate for those who are intended to read and understand it

- have a reasonable standard of spelling and grammar

- use spell/grammar checks and proofread documents

- have reasonable typing speed and IT skills

- share information with colleagues, partner agencies and families as appropriate

- use chronologies and case summaries to create an accessible overview of the case

- ensure that information is recorded within a reasonable period

- appreciate the impact and relevance of key information and conclusions, managing this sensitively and appropriately?

D. Confidence and resilience.

To what extent does the social worker:

- manage anxiety, fear and uncertainty

- present uncomfortable messages and arguments verbally and in writing, giving clear evidence and reasoning

- welcome alternative views of events, challenge and disagreement

- show self-awareness of their emotions to ensure these do not negatively impact on performance

- accept and take into consideration comments, compliments, criticism and challenge

- show confidence in the ability to find workable solutions and make a difference to the lives of families and children

- weigh up available information and views in order to come to recommendations based on the balance of probability

- consult with managers and colleagues in order to reflect on practice and seek guidance

- show openness to very disturbing possibilities and able to 'believe the unbelievable'

- formulate and present information and opinions about children and their families in a variety of contexts including meetings with the children and families, conferences and planning meetings

- resolve conflict and differences as amicably as possible or, if necessary, refer the matter to more senior management

- respond to requests in a manner which allows time to reflect and consider the matter fully?

Capability 9: Professional leadership – Take responsibility for the professional learning and development of others through supervision, mentoring, assessing, research, teaching, leadership and management

To what extent does the social worker:

- influence policy, procedure and practice

- lead, inspire and develop colleagues and other professionals

- supervise, coach or mentor staff/students

- negotiate, persuade, influence and instruct in order to achieve desired results

- manage and develop resources and processes

- use forums to give views and feedback to other managers and agencies

- develop knowledge and understanding of resources, research and theory

- chair and contribute effectively to meetings

- ensure that meetings are focused, fully involve individuals and are recorded, with minutes circulated in a timely manner?

APPENDIX B
Additional skill areas for managers

1. Developing and managing the team
To what extent does the manager:

- promote a culture which aims to deliver the highest possible standard of work
- create opportunities for team members to learn from each other
- ensure that team members enrol on and are able to attend training and learning events
- ensure that fear and anxiety are reduced to a minimum
- find ways in which their team can contribute to finding creative solutions and strategies with cases which are not progressing
- have effective team meetings and learning events
- ensure that health and safety issues are addressed
- manage team budgets and ensure that these are regularly monitored and forecasted with reporting to senior managers
- manage eligibility criteria/thresholds for services
- represent the team as a whole to wider management forums?

2. Supervision
To what extent does the manager:

- offer regular and constructive supervision to practitioners, ensuring that cases are being progressed appropriately and that legislation, regulations, policy, protocols and guidance are being followed
- ensure that workers have a clear understanding of what is expected of them with regards to cases and other responsibilities

- monitor workers' emotional well-being and ensure that they are able to undertake the demands of their roles
- discuss cases and ensure that details are recorded on the child's case record
- ensure that practitioners have an appropriate caseload and that appropriate priority is given to each case
- support and challenge practitioners' values, beliefs, skills and attitudes
- address sickness absence and ensure that the department is meeting its duty of care to practitioners, including making referrals to occupational health and ensuring that work stations are regularly assessed and appropriate
- ensure that practitioners are entitled to work in England and Wales, are registered practitioners and have up-to-date DBS checks?

3. Developing staff and monitoring performance

To what extent does the manager:

- ensure that business and service objectives are met
- ensure that all workers have a completed appraisal every year with a review every six months which considers all of the skill sets in Appendix A
- undertake appraisals in specifically arranged sessions so that there is a clear block of time allowed and it is not compromised by case issues
- ensure that workers attend coaching sessions to enable them to develop their skills and address issues which may inhibit effective practice
- ensure workers are supported on a day-by-day basis and that opportunities are taken to observe the practitioner's contact with families and partner agencies
- ensure that all workers feel confident in the duties they are expected to undertake
- ensure that new staff are inducted into the department and, as soon as is feasible, develop a solid knowledge base of working practices and systems

- monitor all workers, particularly during a probationary period, with regular consideration being given to whether they are performing satisfactorily

- ensure there are professional development plans for all workers and that these plans, with learning logs and details of training, are recorded on the supervision file

- address performance and conduct issues, with action plans produced, to ensure progress with areas of concern and consideration of referring issues to human resources and senior management?

4. Ensuring progress and quality intervention in cases

To what extent does the manager:

- ensure the highest possible standard of practice

- monitor the work of workers and ensure that decisions are taken on all cases in a timely manner to ensure the safety and welfare of children

- make key decisions on cases such as requesting a legal planning meeting, transferring cases, referring to child protection conference, agreeing to a child being looked after and closing cases

- monitor and countersign work, including assessments, reports to conference/children looked after (LAC) reviews, key recording, court statements/care plans, ensuring that these are of a high quality and completed within timescales

- undertake random or targeted auditing of cases

- ensure that work is completed to meet performance targets?

5. Allocating cases

To what extent does the manager:

- ensure that all work which is coming to the team is allocated in a timely manner

- ensure that cases are allocated to a suitable practitioner, giving consideration to the complexity/nature of the case, level of skill of the practitioner and potential risks?

6. Recruitment

To what extent does the manager:

- interview and appoint new members of the team at formal (for permanent appointments) and informal (for temporary positions) interviews using the social worker skill sets as detailed in Appendix A?

7. Responding to complaints and feedback

To what extent does the manager:

- monitor work to ensure that key individuals are satisfied with the intervention and how this is being undertaken, including being part of key meetings, having direct contact with family members and receiving feedback on positive issues/areas of dissatisfaction

- resolve stage one complaints, drafting written replies within timescales which take into account the complainant's concern and attempt to resolve the issues?

8. Working with partner agencies

To what extent does the manager:

- liaise with other managers to ensure that there is effective and appropriate multi-agency working, including communicating with managers in other agencies to resolve specific issues relating to a case or policy/procedure

- maintain positive relationships with partners so that discussion can take place from a position of mutual trust and understanding

- attend meetings and have links with managers in partner agencies so that routine issues can be progressed and explored?

APPENDIX C

Managing incidents of unacceptable behaviour

Preparation for meetings

The outcome of meetings and the safety of practitioners will be improved by good preparation, including:

- being clear about the purpose of the meeting or contact

- giving families reasonable notice of meetings, their purpose and issues which will be discussed

- ensuring that the correct individuals are present to ensure the purpose of the meeting can be met

- ensuring the meeting is long enough to address the issues

- arriving punctually

- clarifying if anyone else is in the house or due to visit

- ensuring that there are no interruptions and that mobile phones are on silent or it is acknowledged that this is not feasible

- restating, at the start of the meeting, the purpose of the meeting

- giving family members sufficient time to state their views

- ensuring that there is the opportunity for a break at least every 45 minutes or more often, depending on what is being discussed and the likely attention span of participants

- informing family members that they can request a short break at any point

- allowing thinking time, even if only for a few minutes, if issues become difficult, emotional or there is disagreement

- ensuring that family members are clear if unannounced visits are to be used and the purpose of these

- acknowledging family members' views and feelings and any areas of disagreement
- acknowledging areas of disagreement and, if not resolvable, being clear about where these issues will be referred
- remaining calm at all times and trying to maintain a non-aggressive posture
- summarising the discussion and issues at regular intervals in a meeting
- conducting discussions whilst seated
- requesting that all animals, which may become agitated, are securely in another room
- ensuring that personal property can be easily found, to enable leaving without delay
- being vigilant about surroundings and potential risk factors
- agreeing at the end of all meetings the conclusions, areas of disagreement and action which will be taken.

Measures to reduce the likelihood of unacceptable incidents

Consideration should include:

- two practitioners conducting the meeting together
- if the meeting is at an office, ensuring that reception staff are aware of the meeting and of any anticipated difficulties
- whenever possible, meetings taking place at the practitioner's office, where assistance can be sought if required
- when using an interview room, ensuring that the 'panic alarm' is working and that it can be accessed easily by practitioners
- practitioners ensuring that they are sitting near an exit route
- if the meeting is taking place outside the practitioner's office, agreeing a time when the practitioners will call an identified manager or colleague
- having a phone number which the practitioner can call to alert a manager or colleague that immediate assistance is required
- requesting uniformed police attendance either in the meeting or situated close by.

Managerial action following an incident

Following an incident of unacceptable behaviour a manager should consider:

- seeking medical attention for the practitioner and others
- reporting the matter to the police
- taking action regarding any persons who may still be in danger
- ensuring that an entry is made on the client database, including management action being taken
- offering the practitioner time off to address their emotional trauma
- completing the council's accident/incident report
- referring affected individuals to occupational health or counselling services
- action required in relation to the care plan for the child
- ensuring that an appropriate service continues to be offered to the child and their family whilst minimalising further risks to practitioners
- informing partner agencies of the incident so that their staff are aware of potential dangers
- withdrawing services
- reporting the incident to a senior manager
- informing legal services if there is a possibility of a claim against the council
- sending a letter to the service user informing them of action which will be taken and the service's expectation of them
- reviewing policies and procedures
- providing feedback to the staff members who have experienced or may be affected by the incident.

APPENDIX D

Contents of letters to families to clarify the nature and expectations of involvement

For all families involved with professionals, the letter to the family should consider providing details of:

- visiting regularity and length
- whether unannounced visits will be made
- the focus and purpose of visits
- who should be present for visits
- other meetings which will take place and who will be present
- arrangements to see the children on their own and with carers
- arrangements to provide an interpreter
- plans to complete further assessments
- plans to contact other agencies and seek information from them
- the confidentiality policy
- how information will be kept
- when information may be shared with other agencies
- requirements for family members to treat professionals with dignity and respect
- plans to review the case
- details of the complaint and advocacy procedures
- the name of a manager to contact if the family are unhappy with how the case is progressing.

In addition, if a child is the subject of a child protection plan, consideration should be given to providing details of:

- the key reasons for the child protection plan
- the category of maltreatment
- when minutes of the conference are likely to be distributed
- the date of the next conference
- the date of the next core group
- the membership and purpose of the core group
- when the report for the next conference will be available
- any requirement to examine children's sleeping arrangements
- any requirement to ensure there is adequate and appropriate food
- other areas of the home which will be examined during visits, with reasons
- the use of photographs, if necessary, as a record of the condition of the home
- the requirement of the family to inform the social worker if:
  - any of the children are harmed, including minor accidents
  - any new child or adult stays at the home, even if only for a night
  - carers of children will be away from the home.

NOTES

1. Ofsted: 'Local Authority Children's services inspection outcomes' (15 October 2014)

2. BASW: Professional Social Work (November 2013)

3. Ofsted: 'Ages of Concern: Learning Lessons from Serious Case Reviews' (2011)

4. Children and Young People Now (7–20 January 2014)

5. The Guardian Newspaper (2 December 2013)

6. Care Quality Commission: State of Care Report (2012)

7. Institute of Fiscal Studies: Living Standards, Poverty and Inequality in the United Kingdom (2013)

8. British Journal of Social Work (1989)

9. National Institute for Health and Care Standards: National Report (2012)

10. The Victoria Climbié Inquiry Report (2003)

11. Social Care Annual Report (2012/13)

12. The Munro Review of Child Protection Final Report: 'A Child-centred System' (2011)

13. Reder, Duncan and Gray: Beyond Blame – Foreword (1993)

14. Unwin and Hogg: Effective Social Work with Children and Families – A Skills Handbook (2012)

15. Seebolm Report: Report of the Committee on Local Authority and Allied Personal Social Services (1968)

16. Community Care magazine (27 July 2009)

17. Elizabeth Herbeck: Workplace Stress and Your Health (2012)

18. BASW: Professional Social Work (November 2013)

19. Chris Beckett: Essential Theory for Social Work Practice (2006)

20. Laing and Foulston: RD Laing: A Life (2008)

21. Prochasta, Norcross and DiClimente: Changing for Good (1998)

22. Colin Carnall: Managing Change (1991)

23. Griffiths and Burns: Engaging Learners (2013)

24. Robert Dilts: Modelling in NLP (2006)

25. Eileen Munro: Effective Child Protection (2008)

26. Burton and Platts: Building Self Confidence 2010)

27. James Borg: Body Language (2013)

28. Max McKeown: Strategy Book (2011)

29. Reder, Duncan and Gray: Beyond Blame (1993)

30. Mo Shapiro: Successful Neuro-Lingistic Programming (2012)

31. Stephen R Covey: Principle Centred Leadership (1992)

32. Rittel and Webber: Dilemmas in General Theory of Planning (1973)

33. Stephen R Covey: Principle Centred Leadership (1992)

34. Eric Whitton: What is Transactional Analysis? (1997)

35. Pam Jones: Performance Management (1999)

36. The Munro Review of Child Protection Final Report: 'A Child-Centred System' (2011)

37. Richard Kock: The 80:20 Principle (2007)

38. Health and Care Professions Council: Standards of Conduct, Performance and Ethics (2012)

39. Health and Care Professions Council: Standards of Conduct, Performance and Ethics (2012)

40. College of Social Work: Professional Capabilities Framework (2012)

41. Jan Horwath (Editor): The Child's World (2001)

42. Graham Allen: Early Intervention: The Next Steps (2011)

43. Vern McLellan: Wise Words and Quotes (2000)

44. Amoeck Van Jawa: Selected Quotes of Albert Einstein (2012)

45. Ratner, George and Iveson: Solution-Focused Brief Therapy (2012)

INDEX

Eradicating Child Maltreatment

Evidence-Based Approaches to Prevention and Intervention Across Services

Edited by Arnon Bentovim and Jenny Gray

Foreword by Harriet Ward

Paperback: £25.00 / $45.00

ISBN: 978 1 84905 449 2

240 pages

Is it possible to overcome the enduring problem of child maltreatment?

In Eradicating Child Maltreatment, leading international figures in the field of child welfare address this enduring and thorny question, setting out a public health approach to prevention. It draws on groundbreaking research and practice on prevention and early intervention from around the globe spanning health, social care, education and criminal justice. Contributors describe what is known about the incidence of child maltreatment, how far we have succeeded in eradicating it, which preventative strategies have been proven to be effective, and offers evidenced recommendations for policy and practice.

Aiming to draw us nearer to the goal of a world free from child maltreatment first articulated by the visionary paediatrician Dr. C. Henry Kempe in 1978, this important book provides new insights for professionals, managers, academics and policymakers across the range of child and family welfare services.

Arnon Bentovim is a Director of Child and Family Training, and a Visiting Professor at Royal Holloway, University of London. He was formerly a Consultant Child and Adolescent Psychiatrist to the Great Ormond Street Children's Hospital and the Tavistock Clinic. He was also Honorary Senior Lecturer at the Institute of Child Health, University College London. He is co-editor of Safeguarding Children Living with Trauma and Family Violence, published by Jessica Kingsley Publishers. **Jenny Gray OBE** is a social work consultant and President of the International Society for the Prevention of Child Abuse and Neglect. From 1995-2012 she was professional adviser to the British government on safeguarding children, firstly in the Department of Health and then in the Department for Education. In this capacity she led policy development on the assessment of children in need, reviews of serious cases and child deaths and the commissioning of safeguarding children research.

Mastering Whole Family Assessment in Social Work

Balancing the Needs of Children, Adults and Their Families

Fiona Mainstone

Foreword by Jane Wonnacott

Paperback: £19.99 / $32.95

ISBN: 978 1 84905 240 5

280 pages

How do you keep the whole family in mind when carrying out social work assessment? How do you balance the needs of adults and children? How do you ensure that children's welfare and safety are everyone's priority when families face complex difficulties?

Mastering Whole Family Assessment in Social Work brings together what social workers in adult and children services need to know about assessment across both services. With tools and frameworks that make sense of the interface between adult life difficulties, family problems, parenting capacity and children's needs, this practical guide will help social workers to think across professional and administrative divides. Case studies, practice vignettes, exercises and suggestions for further reading are included throughout the book to help the reader consider the well-being of the whole family when conducting and interpreting assessments.

This guide will help social workers to think holistically and work collaboratively both with each other and with families.

Fiona Mainstone is an independent consultant and educator with many years' experience of social work in local authorities. She contributes to post-graduate programmes at several UK universities and delivers training to managers and practitioners in both adult and children's services. She also practises as a solutions-focused therapist.

Assessing Disorganized Attachment Behaviour in Children

An Evidence-Based Model for
Understanding and Supporting Families

Edited by David Shemmings and Yvonne Shemmings

Paperback: £22.99 / $32.95

ISBN: 978 1 84905 322 8

240 pages

Assessing Disorganized Attachment Behaviour in Children lays out an evidence-based model for working with and assessing children with disorganized attachment and their adult carers: families whose extreme, erratic and disturbing behaviour can make them perplexing and frustrating to work with.

The model is designed to identify key indicators and explanatory mechanisms of child maltreatment: disorganized attachment in the child, a parent's unresolved loss or trauma, disconnected and extremely insensitive parenting, and low parental mentalisation. The book also outlines ways of assessing children for disorganized attachment and carer capacity, and proposes interventions.

Accessible and practical, this book is essential reading for child protection professionals.

David Shemmings is Professor of Child Protection Research in the School of Social Policy, Sociology and Social Research at the University of Kent and co-Director of the university's Centre for Child Protection. He is also visiting professor of Child Protection Research at Royal Holloway College, University of London. He leads the Advanced Child Protection stream within the West London Alliance Post-qualifying Initiative and directs the Assessment of Disorganised Attachment and Maltreatment (ADAM) Project in over 30 child protection organizations across the UK and Europe. **Yvonne Shemmings** is a Continuing Professional Development Specialist and has trained professionals in over 30 child protection organizations. She is a qualified social worker and was also a senior manager. Her work includes the use of attachment theory in practice. Both David and Yvonne have published widely in the fields of child and adult attachment and child protection. Their title, Understanding Disorganized Attachment, is also available from Jessica Kingsley Publishers.

Direct Work with Vulnerable Children

Playful Activities and Strategies
for Communication

Audrey Tait and Helen Wosu

Paperback: £16.99 / $29.95

ISBN: 978 1 84905 319 8

224 pages

For many vulnerable children, the idea of talking to an adult about their experiences and feelings can be a daunting prospect. This book demonstrates how the introduction of playfulness when working with neglected or abused children helps to build a trusting relationship by openly engaging with the child's world.

The practical activities and resources provided have been developed over 20 years of working with vulnerable children and are proven to help reduce feelings of stress and open up the lines of communication between adult and child. The straightforward, accessible style makes them easy to follow and ideal for reference in everyday practice.

With plenty of tried and tested advice, this book is essential reading for all those working with vulnerable children, including social workers, child protection workers, therapists, teachers and police interviewers, who are looking for effective ways to engage with them.

Audrey Tait is a Social Worker with the Children and Families Practice Team, City of Edinburgh Council. Originally trained as a nursery nurse, she has 20 years' experience working with children in social work settings and for the past 4 years she has been delivering a training course, Communicating with Children, for the City of Edinburgh Council's Children and Families Department. **Helen Wosu** is an independent social worker and holds an MSc in Advanced Social Work Practice from the University of Edinburgh. She has previously worked as a Teaching Fellow at the University of Dundee, a senior social worker for a practice team and as an Employee Development Officer in Child Protection for the City of Edinburgh Council. She currently undertakes kinship care and adoption assessments as well as child development and child protection training.